Let There Be Light!

Hanukkah Meditations

Robin Main

ISBN: 0-9985982-0-8
ISBN-13: 978-0-9985982-0-8

ø1-31-2ø17

Illuminous Tamara,

Your beautiful light simply gets brighter and brighter. Shine, Baby! Shine!!!

All love

♡Robin Main

DEDICATION

To the wise virgins
doing what Yeshua did

CONTENTS

ACKNOWLEDGMENTS

To my family's endless love

NOTE:

Each chapter is divided into eight sections (i.e., days).
If you so choose, you can use these Hanukkah Meditations as devotional readings throughout the eight days of Hanukkah during the nightly kindling of the lights.

To this end, two questions have been provided at the end of each day's meditation as well as kindling of lights instructions and nightly blessings.

1 – WINTER ONE-DER-LAND

DAY 1 - Winter One-der-land

"Then came the Feast of Dedication at Jerusalem. It was winter, and Jesus was in the temple area walking in Solomon's Colonnade" (John 10.22-23 NIV).

Winter One-der-land is a mystery, which God has held for such a time as this.

We shall all be changed. We shall all be gathered together in one according to His grace.

There are many doors by which our oneness will manifest. One of those doors opens at sundown on the first day of Hanukkah. A Winter One-der-land portal of oneness opens, and we all get to choose whether to enter this Kingdom reality, or not.

A gateway of awe has been prepared for this special season of lights, miracles and dedicating our temples to walk as Yeshua walked. *"[22] Then came the Feast of Dedication at Jerusalem, and it was winter. [23] And Jesus was walking in the Temple in Solomon's Porch" (John 10.22-23 Aramaic).* We are told in 1 John 2.6 that the one who says he abides in God walks in the same manner as Jesus walked. We don't have to guess at how Jesus walked during the time of winter feasting. John 10.22-23 plainly illustrates it.

We must understand that our Heavenly Father's timetable for earth is laid out in the Bible according to His Calendar. Its time and seasons always point to the Messiah both in heaven and on earth.

Returning to the age-old foundation of biblical time-keeping should be an instinctive process for all believers in the Messiah.

Biblical time-keeping reveals that Sabbaths sets His people's weeks, new moons set His people's months, and God's feasts set their years (Isaiah 29.1). We will only be exploring God's Biblical Feasts in which the Lord Himself situates a year in the dimension of time.

Every player in the game of sports plays by the same rules. We just need to understand that in the spiritual realm. It's God's rules by which everyone plays, including the devil. When God created weeks, months and years, He gave them as gifts to mankind. His measurement of time helps us comprehend where we are in the process of life. As time goes by, we see our children grow up, and we periodically ask ourselves: "Am I better than a year ago?"

Time helps us see if our growth is heading in the proper direction – maturity.

Hanukkah (i.e., The Feast of Dedication) is not one of the seven feasts of the Lord specified in Leviticus 23, but it is one of the two winter feasts mentioned in the Bible – Hanukkah (John 10.22-23) and Purim (the Book of Esther). If we operate on the premise that Scripture is inspired by God (2 Timothy 3.16-17), we must contemplate why these feasts are in God's Word. The Lord told me once: "Just as the Spirit of the Living God has seven flows that manifests in nine fruits and gifts, so do the Feasts of the Lord."

What society calls Jewish Feasts, God proclaims that they are *"the feasts of the Lord"* and He emphasizes: *"They are My feasts" (Leviticus 23:2).* They have been called Jewish Feasts because the Jewish people have faithfully rehearsed the feasts of the Lord since they have been instituted.

All believers in the first century celebrated Biblical Feasts. It's the Christian Church's primordial practice. If we serve and worship the God of Abraham, Isaac and Jacob; them these feasts are for us too.

The spring feasts in the Bible speak of Jesus' first coming while the fall feasts speak of His second coming. The winter feasts of Hanukkah and Purim reveal the picture of the church's journey until the Messiah comes again.

Hanukkah is not listed as a feast forever, like Passover, Pentecost, and Tabernacles, which are types and shadows of Yeshua's ministry here on earth. Hanukkah is a feast that celebrates the temporal walk of His church becoming His Bride – the two becoming one.

We need to understand as the earth cycles through Biblical time, a different portal opens in the heavenly realms with each Biblical Feast. There's a type of open heaven for a season that allows a greater grace for grace that always exist. For instance, when we encounter Passover in the dimension of time, a portal opens that allows for a greater grace of deliverance.

For those who enter into Hanukkah, there's a greater grace for becoming one with Jesus Christ as His pure and spotless Bride. It's a wonderful path, white as snow, through a Winter One-der-land. It's a time when God Himself is literally communicating to each individual member of the Body of Christ about how He wants our temples (bodies) and altars (hearts) dedicated as holy unto the Lord.

Discussion Questions:

1. What are some greater graces available during Hanukkah?

2. How does the Messiah Yeshua become one with His pure and spotless bride?

*****

DAY 2 – Do Not Judge About Holydays

"Let no man therefore judge you in meat, or in drink, or in respect of a holyday, or of the new moon, or of the Sabbath days: which are a shadow of things to come; but the body is of Christ" (Colossians 2.16-17KJV).

One of the most misquoted scriptures is Colossians 2.16-17. Christians have used these verses to rationalize why Christians should no longer exclusively celebrate Biblical Feasts, or justify why they celebrate holidays with a pagan-Christian mixture in them.

First, of you think Paul would advocate mixture in regard to holydays, you need to crack your Bible open and read the whole counsel of Scripture. Second, please notice that we are told that holydays (i.e. festivals) are *"a shadow of things to come."* Yeshua (Jesus) is the substance; but we must comprehend that a shadow always resembles its substance. Understand when it comes to holydays, we will be answering to the Creator of all things who is casting the shadow.

Believers are not told not to celebrate Biblical Feasts in Colossians 2.16-17, but not to let anyone judge us with regard to them. Meaning we are not to criticize, censure, condemn, or punish people on how they celebrate a biblical feast, new moon celebration, or a Sabbath day.

If Christians used the same logic for the Ten Commandments as we have for religious festivals, where would the church be? There is an assumption in the statement "Don't let anyone judge you?" that God's people are already eating, drinking, and celebrating.

Don't you think that Yeshua would have confronted any corrupt thought of practice in the society in which He lived? Everyone knows Jesus overturned the moneychangers' tables. Jesus taught against the traditions of men. He also told people that just to look upon a woman in lust was to commit adultery. Have you ever wondered why Jesus never told His followers to cease celebrating the feasts that are/were a shadow of Him? Not only did Jesus NOT rebuke the Jews for celebrating His feasts, but He also used them as object lessons in teaching His people about the fulfillment in Himself of their biblical traditions.

Biblical Feasts are God's occasions for celebrating, just as the Ten Commandments are God's ordained laws. God created us to celebrate Him His glorious ways! Read the gospels. Jesus oved a party! His first miracle was at the wedding feast at Cana where He turned 180 gallons of water into fine wine (John 2.6).

The church has not flushed the Ten Commandments. Why should we throw away His feasts –

parties celebrating Him? Don't you want to come to the feasts that the Lord Himself has invited you to? The spring feasts in God's Word recall Jesus' first coming. The fall feasts are rehearsals for His second coming. The two winter feasts are pictures of His church becoming the Bride of Christ. All Biblical Feasts are audio-visual displays of the prophetic reality of Christ (the Messiah). They can only serve to bring us into a deeper relationship with one another and Messiah Yeshua.

In 2 Chronicles 8.13, the primitive root for the word "feasts" (*mo-ed* in Hebrew) is the Hebrew word *ya-ad. Ya-ad* is the term used for when Adam intimately knew Eve. This primitive *ya-ad* root implies that the Lord is summoning His people to meet Him at His stated time, He is directing us into a certain position, and He is engaging us for marriage. My question has been: If we don't do Your appointed feasts, Lord, can we still marry you?

Think of a boyfriend, a girlfriend, a husband, or a wife. Think about them inviting you to celebrate with them; then think about rejecting their offer to party with your friends. That is basically what we do when we celebrate Christmas, Easter, and other religious holidays with mixture in them.

Won't you consider meeting the One who loves your soul at His designated times in His designated places for the purpose of marrying Him?

Discussion Questions:

1. Why should we not judge how others celebrate?

2. Do you think you can marry (become one with) Yeshua Messiah without attending His feasts? How would attendance at His Biblical Feasts prepare you to be married to Him?

*****

DAY 3 - Walking in a Winter One-der-land

"He who says he abides in Him ought himself also so to walk even as He walked" (1 John 2.6 Aramaic).

The Feast of Dedication is another term for Hanukkah. Due to Hebrew being a pictorial language, it can several different phonetic spellings for the same word in English. Hence, sometimes we see the Feast of Dedication referred to as H-a-n-u-k-k-a-h and sometimes C-h-a-n-u-k-a-h.

When anyone asks why a Christian should or world celebrate Hanukkah, the simplest and most direct answer is: Because Jesus did. "*Jesus answered, saying to them, Truly, truly, I say to you that the Son can do nothing of His own accord, except what He sees the Father doing; for the things which the Father does, the same the Son does also" (John 5.19 Aramaic).* When Yeshua (Jesus) celebrated Hanukkah on earth, significantly, His Heavenly Father participated too.

Stop and think about this earth-shattering reality! Our precious Heavenly Father not only approved of Hanukkah, but He joined in the festivities. In fact, the days of Hanukkah were designated as the festival of praise and thanksgiving, because the Hebrews recognized the annual return of the same kind of spiritual force that had resulted in the original miracle.

Christians have been quick to write off the various feasts articulated in the Bible as Jewish Feasts. Yes, legions of faithful Jews have kept these feast, because they have sought to live their lives trying to abide by the commandments given to them in the Word of God.

As Christians, we have been taught that we no longer have to keep the Law - God's commandments – but is that true? We are told in Scripture that God's commandments show us the way of life, show us the way to love God, and are markers that reveal the faithful saints who endure until the end:

- *"[3] And hereby we know that we know Him, if we keep His commandments. [4] He who says I know Him and does not keep His commandments is a liar, and the truth is not in him. [5] But whoever keeps His word, in him verily is the love of God perfected; hereby we know that we are in Him. [6] He who says he abides in Him ought himself also so to walk even as He walked" (1 John 2.3-6 Aramaic).*

- *"[2]And by this we know that we love the children of God, when we love God and keep His commandments. [3] For this is the love of God, that we keep His commandments; and His commandments are not difficult" (1 John 5.2-3 Aramaic).*

- *"If you love Me, keep My commandments" (John 14.15 Aramaic).*

- *"Here is the patience of the saint; here are they who keep the commandments of God and the faith of Jesus" (Revelation 14.2 Aramaic).*

The Church has overlooked some very important details when it comes to being holy, as He is holy. The Bride of Christ, as exemplified by the 144,000 first fruits who kept themselves pure and follow the Lamb wherever He goes, are saints who obey God's commandments and have the exact same faith as Jesus (Revelation 14.4; 14.12).

In that place of faith and grace, we walk as Jesus walked. He walked *"full of grace and truth" (John 1.14).*

Did you know that there are four essential commandments for ALL believers? They are significantly listed three times in Acts 15.19-20; Acts 15.28-29; Acts 21.25. These four essential commandments for all believers prohibit things that had or have connections to pagan customs and/or traditions. These essentials are abstinence requirements for God's people so that they can live a holy life, just as abstinence before marriage preserves the sanctity of holy matrimony.

For example, the first essential commandment's most accurate translation tells us to abstain from "things" sacrificed to or contaminated by idols. SANTA-TIZING Chapter 4 reveals: "Almost every single Christmas custom or tradition is a thing saturated with paganism (i.e., contaminated by idols)."

The abstinence requirements for the Bride of Christ preserve the sanctity of holy matrimony to our Bridegroom – the King of Kings Yeshua. *"[14] Blessed are those who wash their robes, that they may have the right to the Tree of Life and may go into the city. [15] Outside are … the idolaters and everyone who loves and practices falsehood" (Revelation 22.14-15 NIV).*

The holiness requirements for the Lord's living stones (i.e., you and me) are so important that they were mentioned twice when the founding church fathers were discussing what the nations needed to do to become part of God's household. Then, incredibly, Paul repeats them again in Acts 21.25 when he arrives in Jerusalem after his third missionary journey. There were Paul's last days. He topped off his final missionary efforts (gathering funds for the church in Jerusalem) with a final exhortation to the people in the nations to keep the Essential Commandments for All Believers.

If Christians truly want to know Christ and the power of His resurrection, we must walk as Jesus did. He literally walked in Solomon's Colonnade during Hanukkah – the Feast of Dedication. Won't you do as He did? Won't you walk with Him too?

Discussion Questions:

1. How can you walk like Yeshua did during the winter holiday season?

2. How did our Heavenly Father approve and participate in the celebration of Hanukkah?

*****

DAY 4 – Nine Bridal Feasts

"[12] A garden enclosed is My sister, My bride; yea, a garden guarded, a fountain sealed. [13] Your shoots are an orchard of pomegranates, with pleasant fruits; henna-flower with spikenard, [14] Spikenard and saffron; sweet cane and cinnamon, with all trees of frankincense' myrrh and aloes, with all the chief spices" (Song of Solomon 4.12-14 Aramaic).

"Just as the Spirit of the Living God has seven flows that manifest in nine fruits and gifts, so do the feasts of the

Lord." This is the one-liner that our Beloved gave to me about the Feasts of YHVH in His Kingdom.

There are nine Bridal Feasts, if we include the whole council of Scripture. I understand the traditional view that Hanukkah and Purim are merely commemorative celebrations, which is true. I simply believe that the manifested Word of God – Yeshua – elevated them when He celebrated both of these festivals in Spirit and in Truth. Additionally, we spoke about how Yeshua only did what He saw His Father doing; therefore, not only did Yeshua put His stamp of approval on Hanukkah and Purim, so did His Father.

Not one jot or tittle of the Word of God will pass away. The question remains: How does this apply to these nine Biblical Feasts?

Significantly, the number "nine" is the last of the unique digits; therefore, it marks an end or conclusion of a matter. E.W. Bullinger reveals in his book *Number in Scripture* that "9" signifies the judgment of man and all his works. Judgment has been committed to Yeshua as the Son of Man. Additionally, judgment and righteousness are the foundation as well as the habitation for His Throne (Psalm 97.2). Not only is "9" related to divine judgment, but with "9" being the square of "three," it denoted finality in divine things.

Notice that the nine "fruit of the Spirit" in Galatians 5.22-23 flows out of the previous revelation of those things that will cause a person to NOT inherit the Kingdom of God (Galatians 5:19-21):

> *"[19] For the works of the flesh are well known, which are these: adultery, impurity, and lasciviousness, [20] idolatry, witchcraft, enmity, strife, jealousy, anger, stubbornness, seditions, heresies, [21] envyings, murders, drunkenness, reveling, and all such things; those who practice these things as I have told you before and I say to you know, shall not inherit the Kingdom of God. [22] But the fruits of the Spirit are love, joy, peace, patience, gentleness, goodness, faith, [23] meekness, self-control; there is no law against these. [24] And those who belong to Christ have controlled their weaknesses and passions" (Galatians 5.19-24 Aramaic).*

These fruits of the Spirit are kingdom fruits that are only as abundant as our abiding in The Vine. The Lord has conveniently given us a list, so we can inspect the quality and quantity of our yieldedness that produces fruit.

Then we have the list of the nine "gifts of the Spirit in 1 Corinthians 12.8-10 for the One Body with many members:

> *"[8] For to one is given by the Spirit the word of wisdom; to another the word of knowledge by the same Spirit. [9] To another faith by the same Spirit; to another gifts of healing by the same Spirit; [10] To another the working of miracles; to another prophecy; to another the means to distinguish the true Spirit; to another different languages; to another interpretation of languages. [11] But all these gifts are wrought by that one and*

the same Spirit, dividing to every one severally as He will. [12] *For as the body is one and has many members, and all the members of the body, even though many, are one body, so also is Christ" (1 Corinthians 12.8-12 Aramaic).*

And, finally, there are nine plants in the garden of His Bride in the Song of Solomon 4,13-14:

"[12] *A garden enclosed is My sister, My bride; yea, a garden guarded, a fountain sealed.* [13] *Your shoots are an orchard of pomegranates, with pleasant fruits; henna-flower with spikenard,* [14] *Spikenard and saffron; sweet cane and cinnamon, with all trees of frankincense' myrrh and aloes, with all the chief spices" (Song of Solomon 4.12-14 Aramaic).*

The Lord Himself is changing history through a shaking and a rumbling via the full council of God. Somehow the Seven Feasts of the Lord becoming Nine Bridal Feasts in this Kingdom Day is part of the new thing.

Just as our earth spins around its axis and the sun completes a circle every year, so have the Biblical Feast been created for His Bride to *chuwl* (spin), so she (His people) can meet with her Beloved Bridegroom at His designated time at His designated place to become betrothed (married) to Him.

Discussion Questions:

1. What is your favorite fruit of the Spirit and why?

2. What do you think are the nine fruits and gifts of Bridal Feasts of the Lord?

*****

DAY 5 – Let There Be Light

"And God said, Let there be light; and there was light" (Genesis 1.3 Aramaic).

The fifth day grace in this season (Hanukkah or otherwise) is to remind everyone that there's light in everything that exists. Whether one believes in the Bible or not, *"Let there be light"* is a reality.

Ask scientists. Look at the molecular or sub-atomic level. Take a journey back to the primordial *hayah* (i.e., *haiah*) state. *Hayah* is a Hebrew verb that carries the meaning to be, to become, to exist, to arise, to appear, to abide, to rest, to remain, to stand, and to accompany (be with).

In *Exodus 3.14*, we are told: *"God said to Moses, 'I AM WHO I AM.'"* In the original Hebrew, it is translated *"I will be who I will be* (i.e., *hayah*)*."* This *Hayah* State of Being concept is reflected in the three "let there be" statements in Genesis chapter 1:

- *"The God said, 'Let there be light' (Genesis 1.3).*
- *"Then God said, 'Let there be an expanse in the midst of the waters'" (Genesis 1.6).*
- *"Then God said, 'Let there be lights in the expanse of the heavens'" (Genesis 1.14-15).*

Our understanding of *hayah* can reach as high as the heavens: *"He reveals deep and secret things; He knows what is the darkness, and light dwells with Him" (Daniel 2.22 NKJV).* Or our understanding of hayah can be simplified into a Righteous State of Being that resonates at the same frequency in which it was originally created.

God wants everything redeemed and restored to its pristine state, which is the original state that He created. He wants us to go back to Eden and beyond. There is something to mysterious in this notion, so let's dig a little deeper.

When my son was in college, he took Hebrew as part of his archaeology studies. Cody told me that *hayah* is a unique verb. It carries a meaning in the past of what was done. *Hayah* carries a meaning in the future of what will be done, but in the presence tense of this verb does not exist. Instead, it is given that the verb "to be" is just there. It's who you are, like "I Tarzan." The "am" in "I am Tarzan" is already understood to exist, and it manifests in what a person is doing at that moment. This is every single person's reality.

When someone doesn't do what they say, we all know that they're a hypocrite. All of us on some level have been hypocrites where we truly believe that we are something that we are not (presently manifesting).

The Bible articulates that the light within us can be darkness (Matthew 6.23).

> *"[8] Again, a new commandment I write to you, which thing is true in Him and in you, because the darkness is passing away, and the true light is already shining. [9] He who says he is in the light, and hares his brother, is in darkness until now. [10] He who loves his brother abides in the light, and there is no cause for stumbling in him. [11] But he who hates his brother is in darkness and walks in darkness, and does not know where he is going, because the darkness has blinded his eyes" (1 John 2.8-11 NKJV).*

The frequency of our Righteous State of Being can be simplified even more into the lowest common denominator of life – love.

Many years ago, I was shown a couple wonders in the Spirit. First, I saw a ball of knives rolling and spinning through the air. No two blades on the sphere were the same. I asked what this ball of knives was and was told, "Divine Love." As I studied it, the sphere cut through a shroud of darkness in the atmosphere and glorious light rays began to stream through. Then another time, Jesus told me that He wanted to show me something about the Father. These iridescent shards of light began to shoot through the air in all directions. I was looking on in awe, because the beauty was indescribable. Then I heard the phrase: "Just as the physical world is founded upon the waters, so is the spiritual world founded upon the Father's love. Since then I've discovered the Hebrew word for love is *ahav.* Its pictograph literally tells us that love is the Father's heart revealed.

Love is an eternal commodity. 1 Corinthians 13 reveals that we are nothing without love, and love never fails. Take the Winter One-der-land challenge to strive to resonate at the same frequency of the perfect *hayah – "I am who I am."*

In the Hanukkah story, we see Judah the Maccabee and his band of faith-filled men. When Judah and company overcame overwhelming odds as they battled the forces of darkness, they were defeating the things that caused their light to be less than *hayah.* When they choose to go up to the Temple Mount in Jerusalem to clean and re-dedicate their temple, they were choosing to align themselves with a higher consciousness and way then themselves. They were choosing to perfectly be. Let there be light!

Discussion Questions:

1. How do you connect to the Father's love?

2. What *hayah* reality would you like to manifest here on earth, as it is in heaven?

*****

DAY 6 – Shekinah Glory's Dwelling Presence

"And the spirit of the Lord shall rest upon Him, the spirit of wisdom and understanding, the spirit of counsel and might, the spirit of knowledge and the fear of the Lord" (Isaiah 11.2 KJV).

The eyes of the Lord are over the righteous like the rainbow over His Sapphire Throne. He's watching His Word to see that it's fulfilled.

Christian mystics tell us the "Shekinah" is a divine rainbow that radiates colors in two directions. Yeshua walked in this crossover place of heaven and earth at the same time. Additionally, as the Son of Man, Yeshua was filled with the Seven Spirits of God: *"And the spirit of the Lord shall rest upon Him, the spirit of wisdom and understanding, the spirit of counsel and might, the spirit of knowledge and the fear of the Lord" (Isaiah 11.2 KJV).*

Scripture tells us that when we abide in Christ, we walk in the same manner as He did (1 John 2.6). This means that one of the ultimate realities for God's Devout Ones is we are supposed to be made perfect and complete like the High Priest of the Order of Melchizedek. This means we are supposed to be completely filled with the

Seven Spirits of God here on earth, just like Jesus was.

Currently, we are in an opportune time to get beyond God simply visiting us. You know His Presence coming and going… coming and going… coming and going… We are in a perfect time for the glory of His Dwelling Presence to come down and remain. The root to the Hebrew word "shekinah" literally means to settle, to inhabit, or to dwell. God's shekinah glory manifest in His Temple. Never forget that God's people are the Temple of the Spirit of the Living God (1 Corinthians 6.19).

Christian mystics also tell us that "Shekinah" is not found among sinners. The state of our soul does affect how His light shines through our lives. In fact, Ezekiel chapter 8 speaks of four things which cause God's Shekinah to not remain. God first asks Ezekiel, *"Do you see what they do?"* to get Ezekiel to focus on the issues that the Lord Himself is bringing up. Then God adds: *"That I should go far off from My sanctuary?" (Ezekiel 8.6).*

If you desire to abide in Christ, live in His shekinah glory and be made into the exact same image as Yeshua (Jesus); then you must examine your life according to these Ezekiel 8 cruxes for His Dwelling Presence. For more on this subject, check out "Crux for God's Dwelling Presence" => http://wp.me/p158HG-Dx or "The Feast #1" => https://www.youtube.com/watch?v=QbEuq3Tz2Q8.

May His Shekinah Glory shine through you and yours!

Discussion Questions:

1. What would be the benefits to the shekinah glory dwelling in you?

2. Where is God's shekinah glory not found? What does the shekinah look like?

*****

DAY 7 – Heavenly Position vs. Earthly Condition

"Then said Jesus unto his disciples, If any man will come after me, let him deny himself, and take up his cross, and follow me. For whosoever will save his life shall lose it: and whosoever will lose his life for my sake shall find it. For what is a man profited, if he shall gain the whole world, and lose his own soul? Or what shall a man give in exchange for his soul?" (Matthew 16.24-26 KJV).

It's easy to confuse a person's heavenly position purchased for believers on the cross with their earthly condition – a person's current reality in their walk. Your heavenly position is marked with the phrase "in Christ" in Scripture, which is always 100 percent. It's a person's earthly condition that's in process until they actualize being made into the exact same image as Jesus. That is why Philippians 2.12 tells us that everyone has to work out your own salvation with fear and trembling, after we have accepted Jesus as our Lord and Savior.

Nancy Coen points out that when a person is saved, their spirit is saved; but their body and soul are still full-of-the-dickins. Just look at your own life. If your life demonstrates to all the world that you are perfect in every way, give me a call! I want to know you! We can also look at the people sitting next to you in church. Are they manifesting being perfectly holy and righteous? I'll bet that your answer is no.

All of us have a duty to appropriate in our own lives what was purchased on the cross. We need to make it real. We are called to manifest it here on earth. Our goal when we work out our salvation with fear and trembling is for our earthly condition to become equal to our heavenly position.

The blood of Jesus breaks every yoke, but we must appropriate the power of His blood through joining Him on the cross. We must fully die to our own selves to walk in the same manner that Jesus did:

> *"[24] Then said Jesus unto His disciples, If any man will come after Me, let him deny Himself, and take up his cross, and follow Me. [25] For whosoever will save his life shall lose it: and whosoever will lose his life for My sake shall find it. [26] For what is a man profited, if he shall gain the whole world, and*

> *lose his own soul? Or what shall a man give in exchange for his soul?" (Matthew 16.24-26 KJV).*

Denying ourselves taking up our cross and following Him crucified, buried and resurrected is the pattern, until sin no longer has any place in us. Notice that Matthew 16.24-26 shows us that whatever we are not willing to die to in this world will be the very things that we will exchange for the total transformation of our souls into the exact same image of Jesus.

Discussion Questions:

1. What heavenly things are you manifesting on earth?

2. Personal Reflection: Ask the Lord, "Is there anything I am not willing to die to that I need to?"

*****

DAY 8 – Remember to Enter His Rest

"Therefore, let us fear if, while a promise remains of entering His rest, any one of you may seem to have come short of it" (Hebrews 4.1 NASB).

Those who enter God's rest hear His voice. There is a voice that speaks from the firmament when the New

Living Creature of the Order of Melchizedek stands still… when they rest (Ezekiel 1.26).

This voice is also spoken of three times in the Book of Hebrews chapters 3-4:

- *"[5] Now Moses was faithful in all His house as a servant, for a testimony of those things which were spoken later; [6] but Christ was faithful as a Son over His house – whose house we are, if we hold fast our confidence and boast of our hope firm until the end. [7] Therefore, just as THE HOLY SPIRIT SAYS, 'TODAY IF YOU HEAR HIS VOICE, [8] DO NOT HARDEN YOUR HEARTS as when they provoked Me, as in the day of trial in the wilderness, [9] where your fathers tries Me by testing Me, and saw My works for forty years, [10] Therefore I was angry with this generation, and said, 'They always go astray in their heart and they did not know My ways; [11] as I swore in My wrath. 'They shall not enter My rest'" (Hebrews 3.5-11 NASB).*

- *"[12] Take care, brethren, that there not be in any one of you an evil, unbelieving heart that falls away from the living God. [13] But encourage one another day after day, as long as it is called "Today," so that none of you will be hardened by the deceitfulness of sin. [14] For we have become partakers of Christ, if we hold fast the beginning of our assurance firm until the end, [15] while it is said, 'TODAY IF YOU HEAR HIS VOICE, DO NOT HARDEN YOUR HEARTS, as when they provoked Me.' [16] For who provoked Him when they had heard? Indeed, did not all those who came out of Egypt by Moses? [17] And with whom was He angry for forty years? Was it not those who sinned, whose bodies fell in the wilderness?*[18] *And to whom did He swear that they would not enter His rest, but to those who were disobedient?*[19] *So we see that they were not able to enter because of unbelief" (Hebrews 3.12-19 NASB).*

- *"* [1] *Therefore, let us fear if, while a promise remains of entering His rest, any one of you may seem to have come short of it.* [2] *For indeed we have had good news preached to us, just as they also; but the word they heard did not profit them, because it was not united with faith in those who heard.* [3] *For we who have believed enter that rest just as He has said, 'As I swore in My wrath they shall not enter My rest,' although His works were finished from the foundation of the world.* [4] *For He has said somewhere concerning the seventh day: 'And God rested on the seventh day from all His works,'*[5] *and again in this passage, 'They shall not enter My rest.'*[6] *Therefore, since it remains for some to enter it, and those who formerly had good news preached to them failed to enter because of disobedience,* [7] *He again fixes a certain day, 'Today," saying through David after so long a time just as has been said before, 'TODAY IF YOU HEAR HIS VOICE, DO NOT HARDEN YOUR HEARTS.'*[8] *For if Joshua had given them rest, He would not have spoken of another day after that.* [9] *So there remains a Sabbath rest for the people of God" (Hebrews 4.1-9 NASB).*

The Holy Spirit, the Messiah (Christ) and Melchizedek David have all testified" *"Today if you hear His voice, do not harden your hearts."* Let's all remember the common ingredients for NOT entering God's rest:

[1] Hardening your heart (Heb 3.8; Heb 3.15; Heb 4.7).

[2] Going astray in your heart and not knowing His ways (Heb 3.10).

[3] Unbelieving hearts that fall away from the Living God (Heb 3.12).

[4] Hardening your heart by the deceitfulness of sin (Heb 3.13).

[5] Repeating the sins of God's people in the wilderness (Heb 3.17).

[6] Disobedient people who didn't obey God, because they didn't believe Him (Heb 3.19).

[7] The good news that they heard did not profit them, because it was not united with faith (Heb 4.2).

[8] Those who have had the good new preached to them failed to enter God's rest due to their disobedience (Heb 4.6).

But more importantly, let's remember these common ingredients for entering His rest:

[1] The Son of God who is the High Priest of the Order of Melchizedek shows us the pattern of being a faithful SON over God's House, whose

house we are if we hold firm until the end (Heb 3.6; Heb 4.14).

[2] People with faithful hearts who know His ways (Heb 3.10).

[3] Cleaving to the Living God and desiring His will only (Heb 3.12).

[4] We are partaker of Christ, if we hold fast from the beginning of our assurance, and we remain firm until the end (Heb 3.14).

[5] Our obedience shows our belief in what God says (Heb 3.18-19). Or as the Hebrew Shema communicates, there are three steps to entering His rest:

1. Hear

2. Understand

3. Do (obey)

[6] Ask for the fear of the Lord to help you to enter His rest (Heb 4.1), so you will love what He loves and hate what He hates.

[7] Hear the good news and unite it with faith that will please God (Heb 4.2).

[8] Believe God and enter His rest (Heb 4.3), for God is watching over His Word to perform it through you when the right time, place and

circumstances happen according to His heart.

[9] Enter the Sabbath Rest for God's people (Heb 4.3-9).

The Lord is looking for a people who have entered His Sabbath Rest. These people are those in His Melchizedek Army. The *Dead Sea Scrolls* speak of the Songs of the Sabbath Sacrifices that were sung to Melchizedek in God's Temple (4Q400-407, 11Q17, Mas1k).

In this Kingdom Day, the ones who mature to become angelic priests of the Order of Melchizedek will maintain the purity of the heavenly temple through obedience to divine laws, and they will conduit His heavenly sacrificial service.

Discussion Questions:

1. Can you share some reasons why people don't enter God's rest?

2. What elements are included in entering God's rest?

*****

2 – GOLDEN GATE OF MIRACLES

DAY 1 – Eyes To See

"The eye is the lamp of the body. If your eyes are good, your whole body will be full of light" (Matthew 6.22 NIV).

The eye is the organ of sight. The human eyeball measures only about one inch in diameter, yet the eye can see objects as far away as a star and as tiny as a grain of sand and can quickly adjust its focus between the two. Our eyes are two-way windows. They show you the world, but also show others your feelings. Raised upper lids signal surprise. Pupils grow wide with wonder, interest, or fear. You might wink to let someone know you're kidding and perhaps blink when nervous. You may gaze into the eyes of those you love, but look away when embarrassed or ashamed.

Did you know that your fingerprints have forty unique features, but your iris has 266?

The first step to seeing is light bouncing off every object in your sight. The Bible tells us that when we are in sin, we are in darkness and we can't see (i.e., we are blind):

> *" [1] Behold, the LORD's hand is not so short, that it cannot save; neither is Hos ear dull that it cannot hear; [2] But it is your iniquities that have separated you and your God; and your sins have hid His face from you, that He will not hear. [3] For your hands are defiled with blood, and your fingers with iniquity; your lips have spoken lies, your tongue mutters wickedness. [4] There is no one who calls for justice, neither is there any one who judges faithfully; they trust in vanity and speak lies; they conceive iniquity and bring forth grief. [7] Their feet run to evil, and they make haste to shed innocent blood; their thoughts are thoughts of iniquity; plunder and destruction are in their paths. [9] Therefore justice is far from us, and righteousness does not overtake us; we wait for light, but behold obscurity; for brightness, but we walk in darkness" (Isaiah 59.1-4, 7, 9 Aramaic).*

When Yeshua (Jesus) came to Jerusalem during Hanukkah at the risk of His own life to meet with believers, He performed the one miracle that proved that HE IS THE MESSIAH. He healed a man born blind. This man's world of sight was complete darkness until the man from Galilee walked his way.

" [13]And has delivered us from the power of darkness and brought us to the kingdom of His Beloved Son, [14] By whom we have obtained salvation and forgiveness of sins" (Colossians 1.13-14 Aramaic).

Yeshua tells His disciples that the reason this man was born blind was so the power of God would be manifest (John 9.3). We all have been born blind in some ways. Know that our troubles and frailties are for the purpose of the Almighty's power being made known in our lives. You may think that you are in a dark cloud, but God Himself knows our dark places (Job 22.12-14), and He gives those He loves the treasures of darkness: *"I will give you the treasures of darkness and hidden riches of secret places, That you may know that I, the LORD, Who call you by your name, am the God of Israel" (Isaiah 45.3 NKJV).*

In order to return to Eden, we need to see The Judge. The Ancient Hebrew Word Picture for the word "Eden" tells us that Eden is to see the Judge while the pictograph for the word "judge" reveals that The Judge is the Door of Life – Yeshua. He only judges the things in our lives that get in the way of love, light and life. Now, our is to join Him in His redemptive work in our own lives.

Continue to press into Him to have eyes to see, ears to hear, and a mind to understand. Let us return and be healed (Isaiah 6.8-10)!

Discussion Questions:

1. Did you know that you can't see for one-half hour a day? Why? (A: Because you're blinking.)

2. Can you share a place of darkness in your own life where you'd like to see the power of God manifest and light to shine?

*****

DAY 2 – What Do You See?

"Not by power nor by might, but by My Spirit, says the LORD of hosts" (Zechariah 4.6 Aramaic).

The quintessential verse of Hanukkah is Zechariah 4.6. When we, as God's set apart people, purify our temples and re-dedicate our hearts, our light in this world shines brighter and brighter.

Let us look at this powerful verse, as it relates to the Golden Menorah (i.e., Lampstand) in God's Temple from the lowly perspective of an almond. The word for "almond tree" in Hebrew literally sounds like the Hebrew word for "watching."

" [11] Moreover the word of the LORD came to me, saying,

Jeremiah, what do you see? And I said, I see a rod of an almond tree. [12] *Then the LORD said to me, You have well seen; for I will hasten My word to perform it" (Jeremiah 1.11-12 Aramaic).*

An almond tree is a deciduous tree having pink flowers and fruit. Its fruit is an almond. An almond is a kernel. A kernel is defined as a grain or seed; or the central or important part of a subject, plan, or problem. But get this, the seed of the almond is also its edible fruit. What an incredible picture of the Spirit of the Living God enabling us to be able to sow and reap at the same time.

The Golden Lampstand pictured in Exodus 25 is a symbol of the Messiah as the Light of the World as well as His believers being the light of the world. In the Hebraic culture, the almond tree is symbolic of the Tree of Life and so is the Temple Menorah. Thus, we can see an Old Testament picture in the Golden Lampstand of Jesus being the light and life of the world. Jesus uttered this Messianic statement during Hanukkah: *"I am the Light of the World; he who follows Me shall not walk in darkness, but shall have the light of life" (John 8.12 NASB).*

A menorah has seven branches with accompanying lamps. They were called lamps, because they contained the oil and wicks that produced the flame. Significantly, the Golden Menorah's illumination was created by man-made wicks and oil. Significantly, the cups of the lamps that holds the oil for the Lampstand are shaped like almond flowers with both buds and blossoms.

When we associate Jeremiah 1.11-12 with the menorah picture, we can see one aspect of the God's Lampstand. It symbolizes the light of God's Presence watching over His Word to see that it is fulfilled. By the way, full almond blossoms symbolize life while the almond buds represent the hope of new or renewed life. When things look dark and wintry, do not despair. It is only a season for spring is near. The almond tree is the first tree to bloom in Jerusalem in the spring of the year.

Zechariah 4.1 shows the angel of the Lord waking up a person and asking him the same question that we started with, "What do you see?" In *Zechariah 4.2*, the man answers, *"I see a solid gold lampstand … where there is an additional bowl which causes the lampstand to yield a ceaseless supply of oil … "* Then Zechariah 4.6 declares: "Not by might, nor by power, but be My Spirit, says the Lord of hosts." The two olive trees supplying the ceaseless oil to the menorah have been classically interpreted as being the One New Man in Christ – Jews and Gentile in the Messiah (Zechariah 4.13-14).

Discussion Questions:

1. What do you think the ceaseless supply of oil is symbolic of?

2. How can you become a better lamp to the world? (Hint: Matthew 5.14; Psalm 119.105; Proverbs 6.23; 2 Peter 1.19).

*****

DAY 3 – Pure and Pressed Like Gold

"Command the Israelites to bring you clear oil of pressed olives for the light so that the lamps may be kept burning" (Exodus 27.20 NIV).

Let's examine the symbolism of the God's Lampstand in light of Yeshua being the Light of the World.

The Golden Lampstand was only fed by the purest of oil (Exodus 27.20-21). In fact, the oil that lit the Temple Menorah had to be pressed, not crushed. Do you feel hard pressed at times? Remember that the Lord disciplines the ones He loves. To even harvest the olives, their trees must be battered with sticks. Then the olives are pressed or squeezed, depending on its use.

The sense of Exodus 27,20 is that the oil for the golden menorah had to be absolutely pure from the start; therefore, the oil was made meticulously by pressing each olive gently until one drop of pure oil emerged.

What a picture of the care the Lord our God takes in our lives: *" [5] For we do not preach ourselves but Christ Jesus as Lord, and ourselves as your bond-servant for Jesus' sake. [6] For God who said, 'Light shall shine out of darkness,' is the One who has shone in our hearts to give the light of knowledge of the glory of god in the face of Christ. [7] But we have this treasure in earthen vessels, that the surpassing greatness of the power may be of God and not from ourselves; [8] we are afflicted in every way, but not crushed; perplexed, but not despairing; [9] persecuted, but not forsaken; struck down, but not destroyed; [10] always carrying in the body the dying of Jesus, that the life of Jesus may be manifested in our body" (2 Corinthians 4.5-10 NASB).*

Exodus 27.20 says that the Golden Lampstand is to be lit continually. It was continual in the sense that it was kindled every single day without exception, being lit from evening until morning.

Another fascinating fact about the very intricate Golden Lampstand is that it was made from one solid gold ingot. This is not just an average gold ingot, but a 125-pounder, which represents indivisibility. It speaks of a person having one set of values and only one where all areas of one's life derive from the same set of values.

Everything on and in the menorah had to be hammered out of the one gold ingot, including the almond bud and blossom lamps. Nothing could be made separately. Nothing. It would have been easier to make the pieces of the menorah separately, and then attach them; but God absolutely forbid His Temple Menorah to be made in a piece-mill fashion.

You and all of mankind, have been made in God's own image (Genesis 1.26). Even though God perfectly made us as He designed and desires, we are still being formed into the image of the Son. Take heart. The Bible tells us, *"But He knows the way I take when He has tried me, I shall come forth as gold" (Job 23.10 NASB).*

Discussion Questions:

1. Have you ever felt the Lord meticulously pressing out one drop of pure anointing oil out of you? Please tell us.

2. What are some reasons that the Golden Lampstand was made from one solid gold ingot of gold?

*****

DAY 4 – The True Light of Love

" [7] Dear friends, I am not writing a new commandment for it is an old one you have always had, right from the beginning. This commandment is to love one another is the same message you heard before. [8] Yet it is also new. This commandment is true in Christ and is true among you, because darkness is disappearing and the true light is already shining" (1 John 2.7-8 NLT).

Our Lord of Light, Love and Life is Jesus Christ (Yeshua Ha Maschiach). These three concepts of light, love and life go hand in hand in God's Word.

When we accept Jesus Christ of Nazareth as our Lord and Savior, we begin our journey to become like Him, which is also the exact representation of out Heavenly Father: *"[1] See how great a love the Father has bestowed on us, that we should be called the children of God; and such we are … [2] We know that when He appears, we shall be like Him, because we shall see Him just as He is" (1 John 3.1-2 NASB).*

Divine love is the Father's incredible gift to all of us: *"Every good and perfect gift is from above, coming down from the Father of the heavenly lights, who does not change like shifting shadows" (James 1.17 NIV).* The Bible even says: *" [15] If anyone acknowledge that Jesus is the Son of God, God lives in them and they in God. [16] And we know and rely on the love of God has for us. God is love. Whoever lives in love lives in God, and God in them" (1 John 4.15-16 NIV).*

Several years ago, Yeshua came to me in a vision. I saw Him take my hand and heard Him say, "Come with Me. I have something to show you." Yeshua began to explain, "Just as the physical realm on earth was founded on the waters, so is its spiritual realm founded on My Father's love." I began to see iridescent shards of light shoot all around me. I was amazed, especially since I had never thought of what the spiritual world was founded on ever before.

The first thing I did was research if the earth was truly founded on the waters. I discovered, *"For He laid the earth's foundation on the seas and built it on the ocean depths" (Psalm 24.2 NLT).*

The next thing I got loss in contemplating divine love. It would take pages upon pages to even scratch the surface of this topic. So, let's just let the Bible speak for itself: *"[38]For I am convinced that neither death nor life, neither angels nor demons, neither the present nor the future, nor any powers, [39] neither height nor depth, nor anything else in all creation, will be able to separate us from the love of God that is in Christ Jesus or Lord" (Romans 8.28-29 NIV).* Indeed, God is love. *" [7] Beloved, let us love one another, for love is from God; and everyone who loves is born of God and knows God. [8] The one who does not love does not know God, for God is love" (1 John 4.7-8 NASB).*

Discussion Questions:

1. Do you know what the greatest commandment is? (Hint: Matthew 22.37-39)

2. How do you know that God loves you or someone else?

*****

DAY 5 – The Place of Miracles

"The apostles performed many miraculous signs and wonders among the people. And all the believers used to meet together in Solomon's Colonnade" (Acts 5.12 NIV).

Yeshua walked in Solomon's Colonnade during the Feast of Hanukkah, declaring to the Jews that His miraculous works plainly revealed He was the Messiah. The leaders of Israel had previously concluded that when they heard the testimony of someone being healed from the incurable disease of leprosy, it would be an obvious sign of the Messiah. A sign that He had come. Not only that, but the Messiah would also restore the sight of someone born blind. One born lame would walk. This is the context for when John the Baptist asked Jesus: Are you the one? Then Yeshua sent back the message. Tell John that the blind see, the leper is cleansed, the lame walk and the captives are set free (Matthew 11.4-5).

Acts 5.12 informs us that all believers met together at Solomon's Colonnade. All the believers in the Lord Jesus Christ minimally meet in Solomon Colonnade in a spiritual sense when the celebrate the Feast of Dedication (Hanukkah) in Zion.

Additionally, all the passages that speak of Solomon's Colonnade tell us it's a place of miracles. It's the place where the apostles performed many miracles, sign, and wonders among the people. It is also the place where a beggar, who had been crippled from birth, held on to Peter and John; and was healed (Acts 3.11).

Solomon's Colonnade is also called Solomon's Porch. It was built by Solomon on the east side of the temple. From this side, the glory fills God's temple. A porch or portico is a covered area adjoining an entrance to a building. Usually, it has a separate roof. Spiritually speaking, it represents the place where a believer already has entered the temple (i.e., a relationship with God), but not the building (i.e., become a permanent dwelling place for God).

The celebration of Hanukkah holds several keys for end-time believers. Hanukkah is celebrated in winter when things look asleep, just as all ten virgins in Matthew 25 were asleep because the Bridegroom was a long time in coming (Matthew 25.5). By the way, both the wise and foolish virgins are representative of believers.

Hanukkah emphasizes overcomers who cleanse their altars (hearts) and re-dedicate their temples (bodies) to the Lord:

- *"Create in me a clean heart, O God, and renew a steadfast spirit within me" (Psalm 51:10 NKJV).*

- *"Draw near to God and He will draw near to you. Cleanse your hands, you sinners; and PURIFY YOUR HEARTS, you double-minded" (James 4.8 NKJV).*

- *"I beseech you therefore, brethren, by the mercies of God, that you PRESENT YOUR BODIES A LIVING SACRIFICE, HOLY AND ACCEPTABLE TO GOD, by means of reasonable service" (Romans 12.1 Aramaic).*

Discussion Questions:

1. What went on at Solomon's Colonnade?

2. Can you tell us about any miracle you've seen or experienced?

*****

DAY 6 – Ultimate Proof of the Messiah

"[1] The Spirit of the LORD is upon me, because the LORD has anointed me and sent me to preach good tidings to the meek; to bind up the brokenhearted, to proclaim liberty to captives and release to prisoners; [2] To proclaim the acceptable year of the LORD, and the day of the salvation of our God; to comfort all that mourn" (Isaiah 61.1-2 Aramaic).

Did you know that during Hanukkah Yeshua came to Jerusalem (at the risk of His own life) to meet with believers and to also perform a miracle that was the ultimate proof that He was/is the Messiah? Turn to John chapter 9. By the way, John 8.12 through John 10.42 happened during Hanukkah.

On the first day of Hanukkah, Yeshua passes by a man born blind from birth. In response to His disciple's question: "Rabbi, who sinned, this man or his parents, that, he would be born blind?" Yeshua tells us that the reason this man was born blind was so the power of God would be manifest (John 9.3). Just as this man was born blind, our own imperfections and frailties are for the purpose of His power being made known in our lives.

Right after Yeshua declares that this man was born blind so the works of God might be displayed in Him, Yeshua declares: *"[4] We must work the works of Him who sent Me as long as it is day... [5] While I am in the world, I am the Light of the World" (John 9.4-5 NASB).* Notice how Yeshua included His disciples; therefore, this applies to you and me as well.

Next, we see Yeshua spit on the ground. He put His very DNA in the earth, mixed it up, and put the mud on the man's eyes. Then Yeshua requires action from the one being healed: *"Go, wash in the pool of Siloam, (which is by interpretation, Sent.) He went his way therefore, and washed, and came seeing" (John 9.7 KJV).* When this guy comes back from washing in the Pool of Siloam screaming with joy, it's the first time that this man could see. *"Never since the world began has anyone been able to open the eyes of someone born blind" (John 9.32 NLV).* Significantly, Isaiah had prophesied that when the true Messiah comes He will do a miracle that no man had ever done before. He would open the eyes of one born blind; and everyone knew it, including the Scribes and Pharisees:

> *"[1] The Spirit of the Lord GOD is on me; because the LORD has anointed me to preach good news to the humble; He has sent me to bind up the broken-hearted, to proclaim liberty to the captives, and the opening of the prison to those who are bound;[2] to proclaim the year of the LORD's favor, and the day of vengeance of our God; to comfort all who mourn" (Isaiah 61.1-2 HNV).*

Under the threat of death from the religious establishment, Yeshua goes up to Jerusalem to attach a major prophetic significance to the Feasts of Dedication (Hanukkah). Not only does Yeshua do the one miracle that proves that He is the Messiah, but He does it by breaking every man-made rule that could apply to the situation.

The whooping and hollering healed man was born blind drew the attention of the Pharisees, and were they mad! They were so mad that they had wrath in their hearts. You see this man got healed on the Sabbath. This violated the religious establishment's strict rules, so they questioned the guy. The religious leaders found out that Yeshua from Nazareth did a miracle on the Sabbath, and he did it by making mud. It was absolutely forbidden by the Pharisees for anyone to mix dirt and water to make mud on the

Sabbath. It was also forbidden to out saliva on eyes on the Sabbath; then to top things off, Yeshua had this man walk more than a Sabbath's day journey in order to receive his healing. Yeshua was basically doing a huge "In your face Pharisees!!!" What a bold statement! Not only was Yeshua saying, I am the Messiah; but He was also saying, I will break every man-made rule that keeps My people blind and bound.

How sad that the religious leader did not even stop to consider that this restoration of sight miracle had just happened. They were seeing the ultimate proof of the Messiah right before their eyes, yet they were too concerned about people following their own piddlely rules and regulations. They were not willing to relinquish their earthly power to follow a heavenly earth-shattering Messiah. Are you willing to forsake all for Him? Are you willing to go to the Pool of Siloam to be healed of the blind spots that you have been born with? I know that I want to be able to say to the fullest: *"One thing I know: that though I was blind, now I see" (John 9.25 NKJV).*

Discussion Questions:

1. How would you like to see the power of God manifest in your life?

2. Which man-made rules can you think of that the Messiah and His people find of little or no value?

*****

DAY 7 – Golden Gate of Miracles

"[9] Lift up your heads, O ye gates; even lift them up, ye everlasting doors; and the King of glory shall come in. [10] Who is this King of glory? The LORD of hosts, He is the King of glory. Selah." (Psalm 24.9-10 KJV).

An ancient golden gate of thanksgiving and awe has been prepared for the special season of lights, miracles and dedicating our temples to walk as Yeshua did. For those who choose to enter Hanukkah, there is a greater grace given to become one with Him, as His pure and spotless Bride.

Hanukkah is also a door of life that's full of signs, wonders and miracles. If you need a creative miracle, it can be found in the Winter One-der-land where Yeshua walked in Solomon's Colonnade.

The name "Feast of Miracle" is another term for Hanukkah. When anyone asks why a Christian would celebrate Hanukkah, the simplest and most direct answer is that Yeshua did.

"Jesus answered, saying to them, Truly, truly, I say to you that the Son can do nothing of His own accord, except what He sees

the Father doing; for the things which the Father does, the same the Son does also" (John 5.19 *Aramaic*). When Yeshua celebrated Hanukkah on earth, significantly His Heavenly Father participated too. Stop and think about that. Our precious Heavenly Father not only approved of Hanukkah, but joined in the festivities. In fact, the days of Hanukkah were designated as festivals of praise and thanksgiving, because His people recognized the annual return of the same kind of spiritual force that resulted in the original miracle.

The only direct reference in the canon of Scripture to Hanukkah is *John 10.22-23: "Then came the Feast of Dedication at Jerusalem. It was winter and Jesus was in the temple area walking in Solomon's Colonnade."* Jesus walked in Solomon's Colonnade during the Feast of Hanukkah declaring His miraculous works plainly revealed that He was the Messiah.

Did you know that the church, universally, was a supernatural community prior to the pagan feast being integrated into the church's calendar? The assimilation of pagan feasts mixed the holy with the profane in God's eyes and moved His manifest dwelling presence (evidenced by miracles) from His Sanctuary.

For the first 300 years, nothing resembling Christmas existed in the Christian Church's calendar. The first recorded evidence of Christmas taking place on December 25th isn't found until the time of Constantine in 336 A.D. The church followed the pattern established by the apostles. They experienced a life and a power the world could not comprehend. Christ's Church in its primal form, celebrated Biblical Feasts. Daily, even several times a day, miracles occurred. Jesus set precedence when He walked in Solomon's Colonnade during the Feast of Miracles declaring the miracles done by God's kingdom had come upon them.

Recall that Solomon's Colonnade was on the east side of God's Temple. Sometimes the writers of Scripture referred to the Eastern Gate instead of Solomon's Colonnade. Just like Hanukkah, the Eastern Gate of Jerusalem has three names:

[1] Eastern Gate,

[2] Beautiful Gate, and

[3] Golden Gate.

This is the place where Yeshua returns: *"For just as the lightning come from the east, and flashes even to the west, so shall the coming of the Son of Man be (Matthew 24.27 NASB).* Hanukkah is a Golden Gate of Miracles. Now is the time to open our ancient golden gates, so the King of Glory can come in (Psalm 24.7). This is the Kingdom Day to worship God His way. This is the Kingdom Day where His set apart people will cleanse their temples; and will operate in signs, wonders and miracles as a result. But first, God's people need to first deal with the mixture that was brought into the church that cut it off from its holy and pure connection to its power supply. If you want to be part of His pure and spotless Bride, you must pass through His Golden Gateway of Awe that will rid us from all mixture in His sight.

Discussion Questions:

1. Are you willing to let go of all mixture to have a pure connection to the King of Kings?

2. What does it mean to you to walk with Yeshua in Solomon's Colonnade in the winter?

*****

DAY 8 – The Father's Love in the Seven Spirit of God

"And out of the throne proceeded lightnings and thunderings and voices: and there were seven lamps of fire burning before the throne, which are the seven Spirits of God" (Revelation 4.5 KJV).

Today is the day to step into His Winter One-der-land to experience light, love and life in a One-der-full new way. It's a new way in which we will see His word fulfilled.

Not only is Hanukkah called the Feast of Miracles, but also the Feast of Lights. His finger is touching the most important parts of your life, whether they be plans or problems. Cast your cares on Him, and see God work with eyes of faith.

The seven branches of God's Light in His Temple are connected to the Seven Spirits of God. The light of His manifest presence is watching over His word to see that it is fulfilled. God's word shall not return void: *"So shall My word be that goes forth out of My mouth: it shall not return unto Me void, but it shall accomplish that which I please, and it shall prosper in the thing whereto I sent it" (Isaiah 55.11 KJV).*

Never forget that the Seven Spirits of God help the sons of men mature as sons of God. They are our governors and tutors to help us mature into full-age: *"[1] The heir, as long as he is a child, differeth nothing from a servant, though he be lord of all; [2] But is under tutors and governors until the time appointed of the father" (Galatians 4:1-2 KJV).* It's from the pool of the mature ones that the Bride of Christ comes. Everything that flows through the Seven Spirits of God is designed to ultimately bring forth the pure and spotless Bride of Christ.

The Seven Spirits of God was the seven-fold nature of Christ that Yeshua walked in here on earth. *"[1] And there shall come forth a rod out of the stem of Jesse, and a Branch shall grow out of his roots: [2] And the Spirit of the LORD shall rest upon him, the spirit of wisdom and understanding, the spirit of counsel and might, the spirit of knowledge and of the fear of the LORD" (Isaiah 11.1-2 KJV).*

The Seven Spirits of God are portrayed as lamps burning before the throne in Revelation 4.5. They are seen as the seven colors that make up the components of light. Condensed this spectrum of color is the substance of light.

God's very first commend in the Word of God, "Let there be light," set the spiritual foundation of our earth, which is the Father's love manifested in the seven-fold nature of Christ. It is also "in Christ" that all the protoplasm of the universe holds together.

The Seven Spirits of God are part of God's government – His ruling and reigning Kingdom. The Seven Spirits of God are resident in mature saints who bring increase of His government of peace and righteousness (Isaiah 9.7). All believers who mature into their royal priesthood function will have Christ's Being lived out uniquely through them by means of the Seven Spirits of God. These glorious seven-fold spirits promote God's administrated will on earth through the kings and priests of the Order of Melchizedek.

If you want this place with Him, simply pursue it. The Seven Spirits of God as well as maturity for the believer is available for whosoever wills. The revelation that flows unabated through these Seven Spirits of God reveal mysterious, hidden and secret truths of His kingdom coming and His will being done.

Discussion Questions:

1. Which spirits of the Seven Spirits of God are you most drawn to?

2. What are the ultimate purposes of the Seven Spirit of God?

*****

3 – NEW DIMENSIONS OF PURITY

DAY 1 – Gateway of Awe

"[2] Beloved, now we are children of God; and it has not yet been revealed what we shall be, but we know that when He is revealed, we shall be like Him, for we shall see Him as He is. [3] And everyone who has this hope in Him purifies himself, just as He is pure" (1 John 3.2-3 NKJV).

During Hanukkah, there's a specific portal open. It's called His Gateway of Awe. This greater grace can only be embraced through personally spending time with Him in His Winter One-der-land.

I have been asking the Father to completely purify me through the Blood of Yeshua. I received this incredible gift, as I spent time with Him. The Father wants you to know that He is extending the same offer to whosoever chooses to enter His Winter One-der-land to be pure.

Today is the first day of Hanukkah, which is His Winter One-der-land. I saw myself in the Spirit walking on the streets of a crystal city. The crystal was clear, but had a bluish tint. I noticed that even though the substance was crystal, I could not see within the buildings unless I intensely focused on something. I understood that, even though things are private in this place, they are also transparent; because His focus reveals what is going on in the inside.

Yeshua then drew my attention to a seemingly unrelated matter. He had me zoom-in on a tiny black speck. As I concentrated my focus harder and harder, I realized that on black speck represented the black specks of iniquity on my DNA. When this understanding struck me, I closed my eyes and held mu arms our straight from my side. I started to spin in the Spirit. As I spiraled, the black specks came off me – my innermost being – into the atmosphere where they rose.

I felt so clean, refreshed and amazed. I looked at Yeshua who had on the biggest smile. I communicated telepathically and with gestures: "Is that it?! Don't I have to do more work?!" Wow!!! Immediately, I became humble, because I knew that I had tapped into His greater grace to cleanse my DNA.

Yeshua reaches out and touches my shoulder. It's a "light" touch. I sense a "turning on," like when an electrical circuit is turned one. I feel myself "power up." I hear: "Fully human, a living being." I am so amazed. I am in

AWE. Yeshua whispers: "This is your Gateway of Awe, for the Winter One-der-land Season." Wow! Putting on light as a robe!

How appropriate that on this first day of Hanukkah, I hear the one note: Oooooonnnnnnnneeeeeee and I "go there."

Yeshua made sure that I knew that His window of opportunity (portal) for a divine acceleration of one's own purification is available to anyone who chooses to enter His Gateway of Awe during the eight-day celebration of Hanukkah. If you desire to be pure before Him, His incredible offer to cleanse your DNA is now available.

Discussion Questions:

1. Do you want to be pure, as Yeshua and the Father are pure?

2. What does it mean to be fully human, a living being (Gen 2.7)?

*****

DAY 2 – Bridal Restoration of DNA

"You are indeed the light of the world… Let your light so shine before men that they may see your good works and glorify your Father in heaven" (Matthew 5:14,16 Aramaic).

Did you know that Yeshua declared twice during Hanukkah "I am the Light of the World?"

- *"Again Jesus spoke to them, saying, I AM THE LIGHT OF THE WORLD; he who follows Me shall not walk in darkness, but he shall find for himself the light of life" (John 8.12 Aramaic).*

- *"As long as I am in the world, I AM THE LIGHT OF THE WORLD" (John 9.5 Aramaic).*

The second Yeshua declared "I am the Light of the World," Yeshua makes a reference "as long as I am in the world" right before He breaks every man-made tradition that He can think of to heal a man born blind.

There are several dimensions to Yeshua telling His disciples: *"As long as I am in the world, I am the light of the world" (John 9.5 KJV).* Obviously, one dimension is that this statement applied while Yeshua lived on earth; but fundamentally, He was also telling His disciples to recall the Sermon on the Mount: *"You are the light of the world… Let your light so shine before men, that they may see your good works and glorify your Father in heaven" (Matthew 5.14,16 NKJV).*

There is another facet where Yeshua is also referring to time when the Mature Body of Christ on earth will manifest being the light of the world, exactly like Jesus did, with all 12 Strands of their DNA turned-on to be the very DNA of God. To understand the fullness of what it means to be a Shining One, we need to study the entire passage that that portrays what Yeshua did during Hanukkah, which is John 8.12 to John 10.42.

We don't know when Hanukkah became known as the Feast of Lights; but we do know that it was known as the Feast of Lights in the time of Yeshua. Additionally, Yeshua Himself declared "I am the Light of the World" during Hanukkah while meeting with believers, revealing truths about being the Good Shepherd, and healing a man born blind. This foreshadows the healing of the One New Man in Christ who has been born blind in many ways too.

Our eyes are the window of our souls. When our DNA is transformed into the very DNA of God, our souls will be filled with the Seven Spirits of God. The Seven Spirits of God was the seven-fold nature of Christ that Yeshua (Jesus) walked in here on earth. The Seven Spirits of God are the Spirit of the Lord, the Spirit of Wisdom, the Spirit of Understanding, the Spirit of Counsel, the Spirit of Might, the Spirit of Knowledge, and the Spirit of the Fear of the Lord (Isaiah 11:2). Heaven's will and the Seven Spirits of God enabled Yeshua to fulfill His high and holy calling. This will be true for those made after the Order of Melchizedek and Christ's Bride too.

Each one of the kings and priests of the Order of Melchizedek are leading their own inner fire bride forth. There are three components that are always present in the perfection of the Order of Melchizedek, which happen to be the same three transformative agents that assist in the bridal restoration of our DNA:

[1] Daily Communion

[2] Daily Crucifixion

[3] Daily Bread (Word of God)

The Seven Spirits of God filling a believer's soul is a progressive perfection process within the Order of Melchizedek. In Scripture, the deepest root of the words "perfect" and "perfection" reveals the point aimed at as a limit for Christ's full-age mature sons where *"I in them and Thou in Me, that they may BECOME PERFECTED IN ONE; so that the world may know that Thou didst send Me, and that Thou didst love them just as Thou didst love Me" (John 17.23 Aramaic).* If you want to bear His image, you have to understand the Order of Melchizedek; because it is God's expression on earth today.

The Seven Spirits of God promote God's administrated will – His government – on earth through His end-time Royal Priesthood. Anyone who desires to can have this place in Him. The operation of the Seven Spirits of God enables the unabated mind of Christ to flow in the Priesthood of the Order of Melchizedek.

Since the seven branches of God's light in His Temple are connected to the Seven Spirits of God, we can be sure that the light of His manifest presence is watching over His word to see that it is fulfilled. Everything given through the marvelous gift of the Seven Spirits of God is designed to bring the Bride of Christ into the place where she is without spot and wrinkle.

Discussion Questions:

1. How are you a light of the world?

2. What three transformative agents assist in the bridal restoration of your DNA, and how do they have the potential to change you?

*****

DAY 3 – Lion and Bride's Season of Joy

"These things I have spoken to you, that My joy may remain in you, and that your joy may be full" (John 15.11 NKJV).

Quiet time this morning was just that – quiet. Until Yeshua comes out of nowhere. He appears directly in front of me so fast and so close that it startles me! We both laugh! Yeshua gestures like: "What?!" And I can't quit laughing.

The scene changes. He is the Lion of the Tribe of Judah. I see some brown thick liquid being poured over the Lion's Body and on the top of His Head. It's chocolate! With a huge tongue, the Lion licks off the chocolate as it drips down His face towards His snout. I see that He is having fun. Smiling in the process. I get the giggles. I know what a fantastic sense of humor He has. Today, Yeshua is just being silly. He's whimsical. I hear Him say: "Don't forget. This is a season of our joy." More lion smiles. More lion licks tasting that molten, messy chocolate.

"Sweet!!!" As soon as I enter into the "sweet," I see Yeshua morph back into His Son of Man form. He brushes off His hands, communicating you got it.

Hanukkah is the Lion of Judah's sweet season of joy. Our joy is His joy too! Happy Hanukkah!!!

Discussion Questions:

1. How would you like to celebrate Hanukkah being the Lion of Judah's sweet season of joy?

2. Have you ever been surprised by Yeshua (Jesus)? If so, when. (Whether you saw Him or not.)

*****

DAY 4 – New Year of the King

"In the light of the King's countenance is life; and His favor is as a cloud of the latter rain" (Proverbs 16.15 KJV).

A dear friend shared with me that she saw the Hanukkah lights burning the moon in the Spirit. When the Hanukkah lights stopped, the moon was wrapped in a cloud. When the moon appeared again, it looked like crystal.

Here are her actual words: "Today, ascension took me into the heavenly classroom where I was shown Hanukkah. There was a courtroom, but it was closed. The flames of the menorah were burning the moon. When Hanukkah ended, the menorah stopped burning. The moon was wrapped in a cloud. When the moon reappeared, it looked like a crystal. Then I saw a celebration. I was told it was the New Year of the King. Trumpets were blowing. I saw the crystal moon, but now it looked like blood. Then I saw the courtroom was open again. The first thing that happened was that people were escorted in by their angel, one by one, into the court. These men appeared to be in white. Each man was announced to be a king. The court was closed a little longer than usual …

to allow the newness to come. Then all those who had purified themselves during those days were to be declared kings, because they had learned to take responsibility over themselves."

The moon is called the lesser light that lights the darkness in Genesis 1.16. One aspect of the Hanukkah lights burning the moon means that there is a distinct light during this season of dedicating our hearts that the Lord is using to illuminate our dark places: *"I have blotted out, as a thick cloud, thy transgressions, and as a cloud, thy sins: return unto Me; for I have redeemed three (Isaiah 44.22 KJV).*

When this cloud covers the moon' behold, He does a new thing: *"In the light of the King's countenance is life' and His favor is as a cloud of the latter rain" (Proverbs 16.15 KJV).*

The King of King's full life and full favor is now being extended to His Crystalline Bride. *"'Come, I will show you the Bride, the Lamb's wife.' And he carried me away in the Spirit to a great and high mountain, and showed me the great city, the Holy Jerusalem, descending out of heaven from God, having the glory of God. Her light was like a most precious stone, like a jasper stone, clear as crystal (Revelation 21.9-11 NKJV).*

Discussion Questions:

1. What areas of your life do you reign as a king?

2. Personal reflection: What dark place in you does God want to illuminate and redeem?

*****

DAY 5 – Keep Your Oil Pure and Abundant

"But the wise ones took oil in the vessels with their lamps" (Matthew 25.4 Aramaic).

Today, Hanukkah is known as the festival of lights; but in many respects, it is also the festival of oil. Keep your lamp burning brightly and keep your oil pure!

The five wise virgins in Matthew chapter 25 not only have pure oil, but it is abundant enough to be ready when the Bridegroom comes: *"They that were ready went in with Him to the marriage: and the door was shut" (Matthew 25:10 KJV).*

There is so such vehemence in God's heart for His Bride. Can you feel Him chomping-at-the bit? All people who desire pure oil are humble and teachable. They will let nothing get in their way to being married (being wed as one) to the King of Kings.

Let's consider the words of the parable of the Ten Virgins. I pray that none of God's people miss out; but this parable reveals that there are five wise virgins and five foolish ones. The five wise virgins go into the marriage feast with the Bridegroom. The five foolish virgins don't have enough oil and have the wedding feast's door shut on them. Know that all virgins are bridal oneness candidates (i.e., believers):

> *"[1] Then the kingdom of heaven will be like ten virgins, who took their lamps and went out to greet the Bridegroom and the Bride. [2] Five of them were wise, and five were foolish. [3] And the foolish ones took their lamps, but took no oil with them, [4] But the wise ones took oil in the vessels with their lamps. [5] As the Bridegroom was delayed, they all slumbered and slept. [6] And at midnight there was a cry, Behold, the Bridegroom is coming; go out to greet Him! [7] Then all the virgins got up and prepared their lamps. [8] And the foolish ones said to the wise ones, Give us some of your oil, for our lamps are going out. [9] Then the wise ones answered, saying, Why, there would not be enough for us and for you; go to those who sell and buy for yourselves. [10] And while they went to buy, the Bridegroom came; and those who were ready entered with Him into the banqueting house, and the door was locked. [11] Afterward the other virgins also came and said, Our lord, our lord, open to us. [12] But He answered and said to them, Truly I say to you, I do not know you. [13] Be alert, therefore, for you do not know the day nor the hour" (Matthew 25:1-13 Aramaic).*

The Book of Matthew was originally written in Aramaic. Notice in Matthew 25.1 that the Bridegroom AND the Bride comes to the ten virgins. The Rapture Theory is a bogus escapism theory invented by John

Nelson Darby. Do you see escapism anywhere in Scripture? No! The Rapture Theory started with some visions given to Miss Margaret Macdonald. She saw Jesus Christ is going to appear in two stage in the second coming of Christ. I believe that what Miss Macdonald saw was accurate, but the interpretation is not. The first stage of Christ's Coming will be for the 144,000 Bride made up of the children of Israel (Rev 7:4-8). These 144,000 Hebrew souls will be taken by God (Yeshua), like Enoch, as the "firstfruits" of resurrection life (Rev 14.4). The second stage, the Bridegroom (Yeshua) and the Bride (144,000) will come back for the wise virgins.

May your oil be pure and abundant!!! Behold, the Bridegroom and Bride comes!!!

Discussion Questions:

1. What is the difference between the wise virgins and foolish virgins?

2. How can you (as a wise virgin) make sure you have enough oil for when the Bridegroom and Bride comes?

*****

DAY 6 – Divine Light Shift

"Oh, send out Your light and Your truth! Let them lead me;
Let them bring me to Your holy hill and to Your Tabernacle"
(Psalm 43.3 NKJV).

Both sides of the One New Man in the Messiah (i.e., Jew and Gentile) have some traditions of man to come out of, if we want to be one with the Plumb Line Himself. When we hear about Hanukkah, the thing that we hear about most is the miraculous supply of oil to light the Temple Menorah in God's Temple.

The miraculous supply of oil is first mentioned in the Talmud, which are Jewish writings or commentaries that are supposed to be supplemental to the Torah. Both book of the Maccabees in the Apocrypha accurately focus on the re-dedication of God's Altar (our hearts) and God's Temple (our bodies). The recounting of the miraculous supply of oil isn't found until hundreds of years after the first Hanukkah. It's hard to believe that such an astonishing miracle wasn't recorded until many years after Yeshua walked the earth. Personally, I think that Rabbinic Judaism changed every one of the Biblical Feasts slightly to hide Yeshua's fulfillment of them.

Since Hanukkah was called the Feast of Lights in Yeshua's Day and He declared "I am the Light of the

World" twice during Hanukkah, I have no problem lighting Hanukkah menorahs for its celebration. We have to simply remember that the eight-day miracle was not necessarily about the Temple Menorah, but about the eight-day re-dedication of God's Altar and His Temple, as prescribed in 2 Chronicles 29.

The Pharisees rightly gauged human nature when they presented people with a choice between a beautiful menorah legend symbolizing the light of the world and a difficult altar experience symbolizing death to self. Hindsight, institutional Judaism has successfully pulled a slight-of-hand. Most Jewish people and those seeking to "do" Hanukkah right gravitate to the miraculous light, even though it appears to be a myth. The Light of the World symbol is a very good thing, but it's the cleansing and re-dedication of God's Altar and Temple that causes one's light to shine brighter and brighter. Our goal should be to shine with the pure white light of the Messiah, as the seven branches of the God's Light symbolizes.

Discussion Questions:

1. What is the eight-day miracle of Hanukkah?

2. What is your guess about why the miraculous supply of oil miracle was not recorded until hundreds of years after the first Hanukkah.?

*****

DAY 7 – Pure Oil Miracle

"And such as do wickedly against the covenant shall he corrupt by flatteries: but the people that do know their God shall be strong, and do exploits" (Daniel 11.32 KJV).

For the first time in nearly 2000 years, the priests have lit a menorah in Jerusalem using pure oil during Hanukkah (2014). It is hugely significant that this year is being miraculously marked with pure oil that lights God's Temple. It is being called a Hanukkah Miracle. Please refer to http://www.israelnationalnews.com/News/News.aspx/189026.

Hanukkah originated during the time between the recorded history of the Old Testament and the New Testament. Its fulfillment is now also between two epochs of recorded history – the culmination of the Age of the Church and the Age of the Kingdom of God. The Feast of Dedication (i.e., Hanukkah) is Biblical in at least two ways. First, it was predicted prophetically in the Book of Danial (8.9-14; 11.21-35). Second, Yeshua (Jesus) joins the party, which is recorded in John 10.23-23.

The plumb line of Scripture is manifesting more and more in this Kingdom Day. When Yeshua celebrated Hanukkah, the focal point that He celebrated was the overthrow of pagan sun god worship that defiled God's Altar. In a word, the defilement of His Altar is/was "Christmas." People's hearts are equivalent to God's Altar today. Therefore, the first Antichrist's placement of a pagan sun god statue on God's Altar and him sacrificing a pig on it is equivalent to the love of Christmas in His people's heart.

Doing what Jesus did produces pure oil. It's time for the pure oil of Hanukkah to flow. We cannot over-estimate the importance of pure oil, which was produced on the seventh day of Hanukkah. The *Kohanim* (high priestly line) lit a golden menorah in Jerusalem with this radically pure oil! This seventh day miracle of pure oil was announced with silver trumpets that makes a clarion call. A clarion call is one that is loud and brilliantly clear.

If you still want to enter through His Gateway of Awe connected to the Feast of Dedication to engage in a heavenly DNA Cleanse, the clarion call of the Revelation 4.1 door tells us to "come up here!" Come up to the One who sits in the throne to receive purification through the Blood of the Lamb of God.

The miracle of the pure oil on the seventh day of Hanukkah is intimately connected to the Seventh Day Transfiguration of Man for the maturing sons being made like unto the Son of God (Hebrews 7.3). We are called to sacrifice self – our own altars of carnality – on His Altar, which will cause the spiritual DNA of God to overtake our carnal DNA. When our fallen DNA is exchanged for the perfectly pure DNA of God, this is when we are *"without father, without mother, without descent" (Hebrews 7.3).*

Do you hear His clarion call?! Behold, the Bridegroom comes! Wise virgins not only have abundant oil, but it's radically pure!

Discussion Questions:

1. How is Hanukkah Biblical?

2. What was Yeshua (Jesus) celebrating when He celebrated Hanukkah?

*****

DAY 8 – Seventh Day Transfiguration of Man

"And after six days Jesus took Peter and James and his brother John, and brought them up to a high mountain alone. And Jesus was transfigured before them, and His face shone like the sun, and His clothes turned white like light" (Matthew 17.1-2 Aramaic).

It is the work of re-dedicating one's altar that enables the pure light of the seventh day to come forth.

Prophetically speaking, my mentor has taught for years that we now stand in the cross point between that Seventh Day Transfiguration of Man and the Third Day of the Church. It's a divine positioning where literally nothing is impossible in God. With God, one day is as a thousand years (2 Peter 3.8). Since the days of Adam, we currently stand in the place "after six days." There was 2,000 years between Adam and Abraham, 2,000 years between Abraham and Yeshua, and approximately 2,000 years between Yeshua and the year 2000, which means we are standing in the place of "after six days."

"[1] Now AFTER SIX DAYS Jesus took Peter, James, and John his brother, led them up on a high mountain by themselves, [2] And He was TRANSIGURED before them. His face shone like the sun, and His clothes became as white as the light" (Matthew 17.1-2 NKJV). The transfiguration of the Son of Man in Matthew 17 is simply a foreshadow for those who will literally become what they behold – a perfect reflection of Jesus: *"Beloved, now are we the sons of God, and it does not yet appear what we shall be: but we know that, WHEN HE SHALL APPEAR, WE SHALL BE LIKE HIM; FOR WE SHALL SEE HIM AS HE IS. And every man that has this hope in Him purifies himself, even as He is pure" (1 John 3.2-3).* This not only requires that His people see, hear and perceive from an elevated position of the Throne Room, but we must purify ourselves also, as He is pure.

Each of us are a tri-parte being consisting of a body, soul and spirit. When we accept the free gift of salvation by grace through faith, our spirit becomes seated in the heavenlies at the right hand of the Father in Christ (Ephesians 2.6-10). Our earthly circumstances are still lived out in our souls and bodies; therefore, we must work out our own salvation with fear and trembling in our soul and in our body. The good news is that our position in the heavenly realm, which is a gift from God that has nothing to do with works, is quickly becoming our condition on the earth, as we surrender to His will and ways.

Notice when Yeshua ascended the "high mountain apart" that He took the three disciples that were closest to Him: Peter, James and John. The pure light of the Seventh Day Transfiguration of Man is being offered to whosoever will… those who choose to forsake all, but Him, in order to be close and intimate.

Remember that the Seventh Day Pure Oil Miracle is intimately connected to the Seventh Day Transfiguration of Man for the sons of the Living God being made like unto the Son of God (Hebrews 7.3).

During the course of the seven days of creation, God put a seed inside each day that produces fruit after its own kind. On the seventh day, God rested and His Son is transfigured (Genesis 2.3; Matthew 17.2).

Did you know that the seventh day of creation was never closed? The Mature Son of God consists of both the

Mature Head (Yeshua) and the Mature Body (i.e., you and me). It's time for a heavenly metamorphosis for the sons of men who are being transformed into the sons of God. It's time for those pressing in to be gloriously changed into His very image. In this Kingdom Day, if you desire to be pure before Him and press toward that high mark, He will cleanse your DNA. As we behold Him, we will become like Him, and we will purify ourselves, even as He is pure (1 John 2:2-3).

Discussion Questions:

1. Are you ready to forsake all, but Yeshua (Jesus)?

2. What are some ways that you can enter His rest?

*****

4 – BECOMING ONE

DAY 1 – Arise and Shine

"[1] Arise, shine: for your light is come, and the glory of the LORD is risen upon thee, [2] For, behold, the darkness shall cover the earth, and gross darkness the people: but the LORD shall arise upon three, and His glory shall be seen upon thee" (Isaiah 60.1-2 KJV).

On the first day of Hanukkah, we are reminded of the first day of creation where God said: "Let there be light."

An early Midrash spoke that "the tabernacle is equal to the creation of the world," and then proceeds to reveal that Day One of creation corresponds to the Holy of Holies. A Midrash is simply a way to expound on Scripture by going into the text and grabbing principles, concepts and understanding.

Our bodies are the Temple of God (1 Cor 6.19); and the Holy of Holies is where the Ark of His Presence resides within His people. It's the Kingdom of God within you and me, if you will (Luke 17.21).

When we take the "arise, shine" message to heart, we must consider the darkness that accompanies it. Ian Clayton revealed: "Darkness controls the secrets, and kings reveal secrets."

Yeshua is our Pattern Son. In the deep darkness of this earth, the glory of the LORD rose upon Him. Furthermore, after Yeshua laid His life down for all of us on the cross, He first descended before He ascended: *"[7] But to each one of us grace was given according to the measure of Christ's gift. [8] Therefore He says, 'When He ascended on high, He led captivity captive, and gave gifts to men.' [9] (Now this, 'He ascended,' – what does it mean but that He also first descended into the lower parts of the earth? [10] He who descended is also the One who ascended far above all the heavens, that He might fill all things.)" (Ephesians 4.7-10 NKJV).*

Since we have been made in the exact same image as the Pattern Son, we will do the same as we journey unto perfection. The descension process to discover your treasure hidden in darkness is just as important as the ascension process. When I was first "officially" introduced to the descension process, Yeshua called it "scuba diving in the Spirit." He instructed me to go a level deep into myself and look for Yeshua there. Once I found Him, we stayed on that level until Yeshua told me it's time to go a level deeper. He led me to descend into the Kingdom of God within.

The same thing happens with the Merkabah (God's Chariot Throne pictured in Ezekiel 1). The difference with the Merkabah descension is that you go to the Kingdom of God within that you currently operate in. There you look for Yeshua and ask Him: Is there anything I need to die to? Is there anything that is not like you? It's very important to pause and reflect, because this is how the kingdoms of your earth will become the kingdoms of our God (Rev 11.15).

May each of us dive deeper into Him! May we go within and let His searchlight reveal the darkness that covers our earth, so we can arise and shine and give God the glory!!!

Discussion Questions:

1. How do you view darkness? Have you ever found treasure in your darkness?

2. Have you ever descended to the Kingdom of God within you? If so, please share.

*****

DAY 2 – The Heavens Declare His Glory

"The heavens declare the glory of God; And the firmament shows His handiwork" (Psalm 19.1 NKJV).

On this second day of Hanukkah, we are reminded of the second day of creation where God said: *"'[6] Let there be a firmament in the midst of the waters, and let it divide the waters from the waters,'[7] Thus God made the firmament, and divided the waters which were under the firmament from the waters which were above the firmament; and it was so. [8] And God called the firmament Heaven. So the evening and the morning were the second day" (Genesis 1.6-8 NKJV).*

Not only does the Midrash reveal that Day One of creation corresponds to the Holy of Holies, but Day Two of creation corresponds to the veil in God's Temple.

Never forget the personal application to all this Temple Talk, because we are the Temple of the Holy Spirit (1 Corinthians 6.19). The Hebrew knew the veil by the name "life." Just as the cherubim guard the way to the Tree of Life (Gen 3.24), so do the cherubim on the veil (Exo 26.31).

When Jesus dies once for all, the physical veil in the Temple in Jerusalem was torn from top to bottom (Matt 27.51; Heb 10.19-20). Behold, a mystery. There is more than one veil (firmament) that needs to be torn, so that we can come into Christ's likeness.

Yeshua tore the veil of the Temple, so those who believe in His sacrifice on the cross can have access to the eternal reality above and beyond the veil. It's our job to tear the others. There's a multi-dimensional aspect to who we really are and our eternal reality. If we want to truly see the essence of His Spirit in all of creation, the veils within me and you must be removed. Applying the Cross of Christ is key for these veils being removed within us (2 Corinthians 3.14).

During a Mystic Mentoring (in Christ) Group Ascension, we descended into the Sea of Glass (the firmament in Ezekiel 1) where there was an endless array of exquisite colors. The group was instructed by Yeshua to go deeper. We heard: "For such a time as this." Then we all became one in Christ, as His queen. We entered spinning circles of light that we knew was the Door of the Tabernacle of the Congregation. We saw eyes all around as well as the four faces of God: lion, ox. eagle, and man. We saw a whirlwind where everything in heaven was available and we could go multiple places at the same time. At the top of the stairs was a bigger whirlwind with a bridal veil. An angel lifted the veil, and we all came under it. We became the veil. We continued to walk very slowly, as we were touched by the angelic realm in the center of the firmament, and others join us. There is a bridal propulsion where Yeshua and His Bride waltzed on the Sea of Glass. The veil lifted, and we heard: "You may kiss the Bride." We hear another voice: "Who gives this Bride?" Father God speaks: "I do." All of heaven congregated around the Sea of Glass to watch Yeshua and His Bride. A large wedding ring with diamonds all around comes down. We step into the all-encompassing ring and sit down facing one another. We are lifted up and suspended over all of creation. There's a look of delight on Yeshua's face as He proclaims: "And it's all for you." There's so much more. We hear: "Look for the diamond dust," as the wedding ring spins the Bride and Groom into a whirlwind. There's a diamond dust fallout coming from His diamond ring in the whirlwind. It covers the earth. There's a ground level cloud composed of tiny ice crystals. We see a layer of ice around the earth, and a door opens into the Sea of Glass that leads to a huge crystal cave with diamond dust. The ice around the earth is the reflection of God in us, which is illuminated when we come back to earth.

Behold, the veil. Behold, the firmament. Behold, His Bride who hears, understands and obeys the Lord's call to celebrate His Biblical Feasts. Hear He… Hear He… Hear He… The Lord is calling all His people together at a particular place to be married.

Discussion Questions:

1. Why should God's people celebrate Biblical Feasts?

2. Do you see another other connections between the veil(s) and the firmament(s)?

*****

DAY 3 – Tree of Life

"[11] And God said, Let the earth bring forth grass, the herb yielding seed, and the fruit tree yielding fruit after his kind, whose seed is in itself, upon the earth: and it was so. [12] And the earth brought forth grass, and herb yielding seed after his kind, and the tree yielding fruit, whose seed was in itself, after his kind: and God saw that it was good. [13] And the evening and the morning were the third day" (Genesis 1.11-13 KJV).

On the third day of Hanukah, we are reminded of the third day of creation where God gathered the waters together under the heaven into seas as well as dry land appearing called earth. Furthermore, God spoke and the earth brought forth grass, herb yielding seeds, and trees yield fruit.

An early Midrash reveals that Day One of creation corresponds to the Holy of Holies. Day Two of creation corresponds to the veil in God's Temple, and Day Three to the Brazen Laver. According to *Midrash Tadshe*, the Brazen Sea in the First Temple represents the world with the ten ells of diameter corresponding to the Ten Sefirot of the Tree of Life. So, the third day of creation us connected to fruit bearing trees as well as the Brazen Laver.

- *"[11] And God said, Let the earth bring forth grass, the herb yielding seed, and the fruit tree yielding fruit after his kind, whose seed is in itself, upon the earth: and it was so.*

[12]And the earth brought forth grass, and herb yielding seed after his kind, and the tree yield fruit, whose seed was in itself, after his kind: and God saw it was good. [13]And the evening and the morning were the third day" (Genesis 1.11-13 KJV).

- *"[1]And he showed me a pure river of water of life, clear as crystal, proceeding from the throne of God and of the Lamb. [2] In the middle of its street, and on either side of the river, was the Tree of Life, which bore twelve fruits, each tree yielding its fruit every month. The leaves od the tree were for the healing of the nations" (Revelation 22.1-2 NKJV).*

There's a connection between the priests being cleansed by the Brazen Laver and God's people returning to their primordial state where they are connected to the Tree of Life in the garden east of Eden. In Scripture, one of the things cherubim mark is our return to our primordial state before The Fall. Notice how cherubim and a flaming sword guard the way to the Tree of Life: *"So He drove the man out; and at the east of the garden of Eden He stationed the cherubim and the flaming sword which turned every direction to guard the way to the Tree of Life" (Genesis 3.24 NASB).*

The flaming sword of the cherubim is none other than the double-edged sword that pierces to the division of soul and spirit and is a discerner of the thoughts and intents of the heart (Hebrews 4.12). Ephesians 6.17 re-emphasizes this point by declaring that the Sword of the Tongues of Fire (the Spirit) is the Word of God, which happens to connect to the Brazen Laver through the washing with the water of the word (Ephesians 5.24-27).

The Brazen Laver in the Wilderness Tabernacle was made from the mirrors of the serving women who served at the doorway of the Tent of Meeting (Exodus 38.8). These women (who are a picture of the church becoming the Bride of Christ) used to sit at Moses' feet just like devout women sat at Yeshua's feet to learn of the Messiah.

Song of Solomon asks us: *"Who is this that comes up from the wilderness leaning on her Beloved?" (SS 8.5).* Why it's the devout ones who can no longer look at themselves in their own mirrors. It's the pure and spotless ones who look into the mirror of truth of the Laver.

One last note, Revelation 21-22 makes it clear that those who enter by the gates into the New Jerusalem and have the right to the Tree of Life have put off all forms of lying. Please notice that these passages apply to believers:

- *"[1] Then I saw a new heaven and a new earth; for the first heaven and the first earth passed away, and there is no longer any sea. [2] And I saw the holy city, New Jerusalem, coming down out of heaven from God, made ready as a bride adorned for her husband. [3] And I heard a loud voice from the throne, saying, 'Behold, the Tabernacle of God is among men, and He will dwell among them, and they shall be His people, and God Himself will be among them … [7] He who overcomes will inherit these things, and I will be his God and he will be My son. [8] But for the cowardly and unbelieving and abominable and murderers and immoral persons and sorcerers and idolaters and ALL LIARS, their part will be in the lake that burns with fire and brimstone, which is the second death … [9] 'Come here, I will show you the bride, the wife of the Lamb.' [10] And he carried me away in the Spirit to a great and high mountain, and showed me the holy city, Jerusalem, coming down out of heaven from God" (Revelation 21.1-3, 7-10 NASB).*

- *"[12] Behold, I am coming quickly, and My reward is with Me, to render to every man according to what he has done. [13] I am the Alpha and the Omega, the first and the last, the beginning and the end. [14] BLESSED ARE THOSE WHO WASH THEIR ROBES, SO THEY MAY HAVE THE RIGHT TO THE TREE OF LIFE, and may enter by the gates into the city. [15] OUTSIDE ARE the dogs and the sorcerers and the immoral persons and the murderers and the idolaters, and EVEYINE WHO LOVES AND PRACTICES LYING" (Revelation 22.12-15 NASB).*

During this Feast of Dedication, let's all re-dedicate our commitment to speaking the truth in love, as we all grow up in all aspects into Christ (Ephesians 4.15).

Discussion Questions:

1. What connections do you see between the Tree of Life and the Brazen Laver?

2. What is the importance of seeds producing after its kind verses genetically modified seeds?

*****

DAY 4 – Deep Blue Bridal Increase

"For as a young man marries a virgin, So shall your sons marry you; And as the bridegroom rejoices over the bride, So shall your God rejoice over you" (Isaiah 62.5 NKJV).

In the spirit, there is no gender: *"[27] For as many of you as have been baptized into Christ have put on Christ. [28] There is neither Jew nor Greek, there is neither bond or free, there is neither male nor female : for ye are all one in Christ Jesus" (Galatians 3.27-28 KJV).* Therefore, women are part of the sons of God, and men are part of the Bride of Christ. Sonship is about being heirs and the Bride is all about become one. With that in mind, everyone please enter into what the Lord has for you in all things.

The following is a glimpse into one of our Mystic Mentoring (in Christ) Group Ascensions shared by Michell Samuelson:

"She has no fear of the future. The trials just drive her deeper. She has new technology within her, because her very DNA has been changed through communing with Him… the very desire she is consumed with. A fire goes before her and burns up her enemies. The light of God becomes a city and wherever she goes she brings the dance, and the city falls in step with the King of Kings and the Lord of Lords who is above all and worthy of all praise, attention and adoration. The increase is on. We are in a season of INCREASE."

Discussion Questions:

1. What are the benefits of being sons and heirs?

2. What are the benefits of being Christ's Bride and being one with Him?

*****

DAY 5 – Bridal DNA Dance

"Then shall the virgin rejoice in the dance, And young men and the old, together; For I will turn their mourning to joy, Will comfort them, and make them rejoice rather than sorrow" (Jeremiah 31.13 Aramaic).

Come to His dance floor. Sway back and forth to the rhythms of restorative peace. This dance is about becoming one. The more transparent we are, the easier it is to become one with Christ and with one another.

Let Yeshua infuse your sword and your shield with His blood. Become encapsulated in Him. Become purified through the flashing, whirling and spinning blood cleansing of our DNA. Let your DNA be changed into a new technology, and become one it in.

Hanukkah is a Winter One-Der-Land mystery that God has reserved for such a time as this. It is a Gateway of Awe. Hanukkah is a portal of oneness that opens to this greater grace to whosoever wills.

The one who abides in God walks in the same manner that Jesus walked: *"[22]And IT WAS AT JERUSALEM THE FEAST OF DEDICATION, and it was winter. [23]And JESUS WALKED IN THE TEMPLE IN SOLOMON'S PORCH" (John 10.22-23 KJV).* We do not have to guess how Jesus walked during the winter feasting season. It is starkly evident that Yeshua celebrated Hanukkah, not Christmas. Selah.

Here comes His Bride all dressed in white moving to the rhythms of His Word and Grace.

Discussion Questions:

1. What have been some of your dance steps with the King of Kings?

2. What exactly is oneness with Christ? How does transparency help oneness?

*****

DAY 6 – Diamond Bridal Jubilee

"But the wise took oil in their vessels with their lamps" (Matthew 25.4 KJV).

Behold, the wise virgins with their lamps of oil. The eternal light of the wise virgins is now being deposited into the Bride of Christ's very core. A light shoots up from her core in a helix formation directing all praise, honor and power to Him. Don't let people misdirect your steps.

Hear the Beloved's heart: "I want you to lavish on

Me, Illuminated Ones." Let your laser focus go up and come together into one shaft of light. Yeshua is the center of His wise virgins' focus. We all merge together in His light. We all lay down and mutually submit to Him.

The stakes are high. All of heaven is watching and desiring this. Yeshua's heart is that more people would take position of being focused, surrendered and in tune with YHVH.

Behold, in this year of diamond jubilee, His Bride is being clothed in a diamond-encrusted dress. She is encapsulated in the ring of His love. In the Bridal Chamber under His wedding *chupa* everything is draped in His designer diamonds. His Bride is made up of wise virgins. His Bride contains it all. Being made into His exact image, we contain all the secrets of the kingdom and the mysteries hidden from the ages.

Discussion Questions:

1. Can you think of a mystery that has been hidden from the ages? (Hint: Look up "mystery" or "mysteries" in Scripture.)

2. Why is being focused and surrendered key to the transformation of His Bridal Company?

*****

DAY 7 – Here Comes His Golden Bride

"But we have this treasure in earthen vessels, that the excellence of the power may be of God and not of us" (2 Corinthians 4.7 NKJV).

We have these treasures in earthen vessels, but never forget that we have also been made in God's image – divine.

Behold, a large golden bird with a beak of gold and fire in his eyes. Hear his loud screech that fills the air putting the whole earth on notice. Understand. Here comes His Golden Bride!

His Golden Bride has a frequency that's purely synchronized with YHVH. God is literally burning up distortion and distraction. Distortion is distracting from the singular upward golden sword focus.

Let all impurities be stirred up, and come to the top of His molten gold, so they can go poof and be gone.

Discussion Questions:

1. How are you coming forth as gold? What difficulties are you overcoming?

2. What will be the result of His Golden Bride being purely synchronized with YHVH?

*****

DAY 8 – Marriage Contract

"Speak to the children of Israel and say to them, Concerning the feasts of the Lord which you shall proclaim to be holy convocations, these are My feasts" (Leviticus 23.2 Aramaic).

Won't you celebrate the King of Kings? The root meaning to the word "feast" in 2 Chronicles 8.13 tells us that at God's Appointed Feasts (those that are in His Word), He is calling us together at a particular time to a particular place, so we can marry Him.

Can't you hear Him calling devout hearts everywhere? Can you hear Him saying: Won't you come to Me? Won't you join Me at My Feast where My Table is set (Lev 23.2; 1 Cor 10.21)?

At the same time that Aaron made an altar according to God's specs, took the people's gold, and made a golden calf idol, Moses received the nation's *ketubah* (i.e., marriage contract) on the mountain of God. God's side of the *ketubah* was Him giving the Ten Commandments.

The number "8" in Scripture signifies a new beginning. Therefore, it's very appropriate on the eighth and final day of Hanukkah to consider what we are choosing this day. Are you choosing the Golden Calf (i.e., Christmas)? Or are you choosing His Marriage Contract, which lines up with celebrating God's Feasts His way?

Jesus celebrated Hanukkah, not Christmas. Hanukkah is all about overthrowing an Antichrist and his polluted sun god sacrifices placed on God's Altar, which is essentially Christmas. Unbeknownst to most Christians, we have actually been doing what the first named Antichrist did and have been calling it true worship. In 168 B.C. on December 25th, Antiochus Epiphanes IV set up a statue of a pagan sun god on the Brazen Altar in God's Temple to be worshiped; and then, he sacrificed a pig on that same altar.

Our bodies are the temple of the Holy Spirit and our hearts are His Ultimate Altar. Believers have lost track of the fact that throughout antiquity all the pagan sun gods' birthdays were celebrated on the ancient winter solstice – December 25th – equivalent to our modern Christmas Day.

To make matters worse, the immediate predecessor of our modern Christmas Season can be literally traced back to the Golden Calf that Aaron fashioned. For more information, please refer to the "North Pole Going South?" article => http://wp.me/p158HG-kH.

His heart is calling every heart everywhere to join Yeshua's bridal celebration at the Lord's Table – the Wedding Supper of the Lamb. Won't you accept His invitations that are resident in His Biblical Feasts?

Discussion Questions:

1. Did you know that the invitation to the Marriage Super of the Lamb is resident in accepting His invitation to His Biblical Feasts? Why do you think that makes sense, or not?

2. Why did Jesus celebrate Hanukkah, not Christmas?

*****

5 - OVERSHADOWING MESSIANIC LIGHT

"Let no man therefore judge you … in respect of a holy day … which are a shadow of things to come; but the body is of Christ" (Colossians 2:16-17 KJV).

The lights of Hanukkah are overshadowing everyone's Winter One-Der-Land this year. This eternal reality was especially illustrated during the 2016 Hanukkah Season. The Feast of Dedication began at sundown on December 24, 2016 and ended sundown January 1, 2017.

"[16] Let no man therefore judge you in regard … to a festival or a new moon or a Sabbath day – [17] things which are a mere shadow of what is to come; but the substance belongs to Christ" (Colossians 2.16-17 NASB). Even though Biblical Feasts are precious components of His Word, they are only *"a mere shadow of what is to come."* Messiah Yeshua is the substance behind all the Biblical Feasts.

The spring feasts in the Bible speak of Jesus' first coming and the fall feasts speak of His second coming. The two winter feasts mentioned in the Word of God – Hanukkah and Purim – portray God's people's journey to becoming His Bride. "Just as the Spirit of the Living God has seven flows that manifests in nine fruits and gifts, so do the Feasts of the Lord." This is the one-liner God gave me regarding the Feasts of the Lord in His Kingdom.

Just as our earth spins around its axis and the sun in a complete circle every year, so have the Biblical Feasts been created for His Bride to *chuwl* (spin), so His people can be woven into a tapestry of love through meeting with God at His designated time(s) and His designated place(s). God's people will literally embody the marks of time: *"Let no man therefore judge you … in respect of a holy day … which are a shadow of things to come; but* THE BODY IS OF CHRIST*" (Colossians 2.16-17 KJV).*

Do you know which aspect of the Lord has put in place the marks of His time. It's the keeper of time – Metatron – who is the fullness of God bodily. The righteous reality of Metatron is that Metatron is the undifferentiated state of the Messiah, which is made up of the Mature Head of Yeshua and the fully mature members of His Body. When Scripture says that the marks of time that set His people's years, months and weeks (festival, new moon, Sabbath) are "shadow of things to come," know that God created man as His shadow. When God created man in His own divine image, the Hebrew word *tzelem* is used and is derived from *tzel*, which means "shadow."

Therefore, one of the glorious interpretations of a "shadow of things to come" is the Body of Christ becoming the perfectly pure manifestation of the fully mature One New Man in Christ (Messiah) - Metatron. See Ephesians 2.15 and Ephesians 4.13. This is the Messianic Light of Hanukkah overshadowing God's Winter One-der-land of the world.

May the overshadowing light and love of the Messianic Light of Hanukkah enlighten you and bless you now and forever more.

DAY 1 – The Light Has Come

"And this is the judgment, that light has come into the world and yet men have loved darkness more than light, because their works were evil" (John 3.19 Aramaic).

I asked Yeshua what He'd like to share on the first night of Hanukkah, and He is simply saying, "The light has come."

- *"[19] This is the judgment, that the Light has come into the world, and men loved the darkness rather than the Light, for their deeds were evil. [20] For everyone who does evil hates the Light, and does not come to the Light for fear that his deeds will be exposed. [21] But he who practices the truth comes to the Light, so that his deeds may be manifested as having been wrought in God" (John 3.19-21 NASB).*

- *"[35] So Jesus said to them, 'For a little while longer the Light is among you. Walk while you have the Light, so that darkness will not overtake you; he who walks in darkness does not know where he goes. [36] While you have the Light, believe in the Light, so that you may become sons of Light.' These things Jesus spoke, and He went away and hid Himself from them" (John 12.35-36 NASB).*

- *"Therefore do not go on passing judgment before the time, but wait until the Lord comes who will both bring to light the things hidden in the darkness and disclose the motives of men's hearts; and then each man's praise will come to him from God" (1 Corinthians 4.5 NASB).*

Discussion Questions:

1. What does "the light has come" mean to you?

2. How do you become a Son of Light?
   (Hint: See John 12.36)

*****

DAY 2 – The Witness of the Light of the Messiah

"There were seven lamps of fire burning before the throne, which are the seven Spirits of God" (Revelation 4.5 KJV).

The second day of Hanukkah testifies of a witness – the witness of the Light of the Messiah. The seven-branched lights in God's Temple are connected to the Seven Spirits of God and to the seven-fold nature of Jesus Christ. This is the witness of the Light of the Messiah:

- *"[1] And there shall come forth a rod out of the stem of Jesse, and a Branch shall grow out of his roots: [2] And the Spirit of the LORD shall rest upon him, the spirit of wisdom and understanding, the spirit of counsel and might, the spirit of knowledge and of the fear of the Lord" (Isaiah 11.1-2 KJV).*

- *"There were seven lamps of fire burning before the throne, which are the seven Spirits of God" (Revelation 4.5 KJV).*

- *"[10] I was in the Spirit on the Lord's Day, and I heard behind me a loud voice, as a trumpet, [11] saying, 'I am the Alpha and the Omega, the First and the Last … [12] Then I turned to see the voice that spoke with me. And having turned I saw golden lampstands, [13] and in the midst of the seven lampstands One like the Son of Man, clothed with a garment down to the feet and girded about the chest with a*

> *golden band.* [14] *His head and hair were like wool, as white as snow, and His eyes like a flame of fire" (Revelation 1.10-14* NKJV*).*

The witness of the Light of the Messiah resides in Melchizedek saints who will have Christ's being lived out through them by means of the Seven Spirits of God. Walking in the same manner as Jesus did is both an internal and external work. The Seven Spirits of God are part of the government of God that's resident in the mature sons of the Most High God. When our DNA is transformed into the very DNA of God, our souls will be filled with the Seven Spirits of God. The Seven Spirits of God is the seven-fold nature of Christ that Yeshua (Jesus) walked in here on earth.

Revelation chapter 1 starts out with: *"*[1] *The revelation of Jesus Christ, which God gave Him to show His servants ...* [4] *Grace to you and peace from Him who is and who was and who is to come, and from the seven Spirits who are before the throne,* [5] *and from Jesus Christ, the faithful witness" (Revelation 1.1, 4-5* NKJV*).* The faithful witness Jesus Christ is one with Father God who is and who was and who is to come and the seven flows of the Holy Spirit.

The seven spirits of God can be seen as seven colors, which are the components of light:

[1] The Spirit of the Lord – red

[2] The Spirit of Wisdom – orange

[3] The Spirit of Understanding – yellow

[4] The Spirit of Counsel – unusual green

[5] The Spirit of Might (Power) – light blue

[6] The Spirit of Knowledge – indigo

[7] The Spirit of the Fear of the Lord – violet

Condensed this spectrum of color is the substance of light. The first command in Scripture set the spiritual foundation of our earth – "Let there be light." The Father's love manifests in the seven-fold nature of Christ; and "in Christ," all the protoplasm of the universe holds together. This truly is the Light of the World! The Father's love manifest in the Seven Spirits of God.

The Seven Spirits of God are part of the Father's ruling and reigning Kingdom. As mentioned previously, the Seven Spirits of God are resident in mature saints who bring increase of His government and peace (Isaiah 9.7). The full sphere of the government of God is revealed by the Father's will, which includes the Spirit of the Lord, spirit of wisdom and understanding, the spirit of counsel and might, the spirit of knowledge and the reverential and obedient fear of the Lord (Isaiah 11.2). This literally is the light of the Messiah whose eyes search to and fro seeking for the hearts that are truly His:

- *"And I looked, and behold, in the midst of the throne and of the four living creatures, and in the midst of the elders, stood a Lamb as though it had been slain, having seven horns and seven eyes, which are the seven Spirits of God sent out into all the earth" (Revelation 5.6 NKJV).*

- *"[7] Thus says the LORD of hosts: 'If you will walk in My ways, And if you will keep My command, Then you shall also judge My house, And likewise have charge of My courts; I will give you places to walk Among these who stand here. [8] Hear. O Joshua, the High Priest, You and your companions who sit before you, For they are a wondrous sign; For behold, I am bringing forth My Servant the BRANCH. [9] For behold, the stone That I have laid before Joshua: Upon the stone are seven eyes" (Zechariah 3.7-9 NKJV).*

Discussion Questions:

1. How are you a witness to the Light of the Messiah?

2. What part does getting to know the Father's will and love has in the restoration of all things?

*****

DAY 3 – Complete Restoration of DNA

"And the LORD God formed Adam out of the soil of the earth, and breathed into his nostrils the breath of life; and man became a living being" (Genesis 2.7 Aramaic).

The third day of Hanukkah reveals the connection between the Feast of Dedication and the complete restoration of our DNA into the very DNA of God.

Yeshua declared twice during Hanukkah "I am Light of the World." This gives us some insightful clues for us fully becoming "the light of the world" (Matt 5.14). Within Hanukkah are several profound mysteries of Christ and His Kingdom that have been hidden for such a time as this.

Some of the most profound mysteries are hidden within the history of Hanukkah itself. Once Judah the Maccabee and his band of faithful men took their courageous stand against the Antichrist of their day, their first priority when they took the Temple Mount was removing the stones of the defiled altar and quickly constructing a new one, so the daily burnt offerings could begin the next morning. The original eight days of the very first Hanukkah in 165 B.C. was the eight days it took to sanctify and cleanse the House of the Lord, which required daily burnt offerings on the Burnt Altar (2 Chronicles 29).

To return to our primordial Living Being of Light State, we must tear down any defiled altars in our hearts and reconstruct new ones. Then our daily burnt offerings (daily taking up our crosses and following Him) can lead us to fully present our bodies as holy and pleasing living sacrifices (Romans 12.1). Before the Fall, human beings were called "living beings" (Genesis 2.7). They had all 12 strands of their DNA actively working, which completely consisted of light. After the Fall, 10 strands of DNA were deactivated and have remained largely dormant until now. These ten shadow strands of DNA have been called "junk DNA."

Connected to the ten shadow strands of DNA are the Ten Copper Chariot Lavers in Solomon's Temple. Just as the Ten Copper Chariot Lavers were dismantled, taken captive by Babylon and treated like junk, so has our ten shadow strands of DNA.

Know that the "chariot" in the Ten Copper Chariot Lavers is the Merkabah process where each of us must descend to the Kingdom of God within to examine ourselves before we ascend in Christ. The *Merkabah* is God's Chariot Throne as portrayed in Ezekiel chapter 1. The *Merkabah* descension process is equivalent to the daily burnt offering process. Both are intended for true introspection where we can see if the kingdoms of our earth align with His Kingdom. Once we truly see the current reality in which we operate with YHVH's eyes, we need to make necessary adjustment in order to be one with the plumb line – Messiah Yeshua. Know that the Great Shepherd of our soul chose what best crucifies our sin nature.

Also, know that these Ten Copper Chariot Lavers were used to wash the blood from the burnt offerings. The Ten Copper Chariot Lavers could not wash the burnt offerings until they were properly prepared, as God prescribed. How do we properly prepare ourselves daily, as a living sacrifice to burn up our sin nature, as a burnt offering.

Remember that there are three components always present in the perfection of the Order of Melchizedek, which are the same transformative agents that accomplishes the bridal restoration of our DNA:

[1] Daily Communion

[2] Daily Crucifixion

[3] Daily Bread (i.e., Word of God)

May your DNA be completely restored into it original divine design (Genesis 1.26-27)!

Discussion Questions:

1. What ways have you followed Jesus Christ death, burial and resurrection?

2. What is the goal of the descension process of the Merkabah? (Hint: Matthew 16.24-26)

*****

DAY 4 – You are the Light of the World

"[14] You are indeed the light of the world; a city that is built upon a mountain cannot be hidden. [16] Let your light so shine before men that they may see your good works and glorify your Father in heaven" (Matthew 5.14,16 Aramaic).

Just as the Messianic lights of Hanukkah get brighter, so are we getting brighter as the light of the world (Matthew 5.14). The fourth day of Hanukkah celebrates our light becoming divine again. One day (perhaps sooner than we think) Messiah Yeshua will have a mature body literally manifesting the exact brilliance as the Light of the World – Yeshua – with all 12 Strands of our DNA turned on.

When our DNA is transformed into the DNA of God, our souls will be filled with the Seven Spirits of God. Recall that the Seven Spirits of God was the seven-fold nature of Christ that Yeshua walked in here on earth (Isaiah 11.1-2).

Recall that the three components always present in the perfection of the Order of Melchizedek are the same transformative agents that accomplished the bridal restoration of our DNA:

[1] Daily Communion

[2] Daily Crucifixion

[3] Daily Bread (Word)

The ultimate goal of daily communion, daily crucifixion and daily bread is to completely re-dedicate our hearts in such a way that we become His Shining Ones where we take on our cherubic nature that was "divine" in the beginning (Genesis 1.26-27).

DAILY COMMUNION causes our bones to start producing the correct record in our blood first. Then, as we make the right choices to line-up with God's Word (i.e., DAILY BREAD), our bodies get conformed into His image that has been born in our blood first. Conveniently, DAILY CRUCIFIXION is included in daily communion, because genuine partaking of communion requires us to examine our hearts and behaviors. This is the Merkabah (God's Chariot Throne) descension process previously discussed.

Never forget that once our bones produce His record in our blood, we must rightly examine the current reality we operate out of in order to be conformed into His image (body, soul and spirit). This is how God's people literally "present your bodied a living sacrifice, holy, acceptable unto God" (Romans 12.1). Therefore, when God takes out your stony heart of flesh and gives you a new heart of flesh, the Lord deposits the original seed that has the potential to be transformed into Jesus' exact same image.

Once the burnt offering gets slaughtered, the blood gets washed by the water of the word and the washing of regeneration and renewing of the Spirit in the Ten Copper Chariot Lavers. In other words, daily crucifixion of our sin nature will cause our Ten Shadow Strands of DNA to be cleansed. In fact, Matthew 16.26 reveals that the things of the world that we will not die to are the very things that we are exchanging for the total transformation of our soul. Our transfiguration into being Sons of Light will be clearly seen. Everyone will know who has their 12 Stands of DNA fully turned on.

May you and yours manifest being His Shining Ones!!!

Discussion Questions:

1. Do you take daily communion? If so, what benefits have your seen?

2. Do you daily die to yourself and your own ways, as a continual burnt offering on God's Altar? Do you find it easy or hard to do?

*****

DAY 5 – The Hebrew Living Letters Connection to "Let There Be Light"

"[3] Then God said, 'Let there be light'; and there was light. [4] And God saw the light, that it was good; and God divided the light from the darkness" (Genesis 1:3-4 NKJV).

On the fifth day of Hanukkah, let us celebrate the completely perfect light God created in the beginning, which is the essence of all God-given light in the cosmos.

"[3] Then God said, 'Let there be light'; and there was light. [4] And God saw the light, that it was good; and God divided the light from the darkness" (Genesis 1:3-4 NKJV). "Let there be light" is the first declaration of God's will in Scripture, but He could not have spoken His will without first creating a language to communicate His thoughts. The human need to formulate our thoughts into language emulates how the Lord spoke in the beginning. Before God spoke the universe into existence, He first created the language to speak forth His will. *"You are worthy, O Lord, To receive glory and honor and power; For You created all things, And by Your will they exist and were created" (Revelation 4.11 NKJV).*

A fundamental concept for Jewish mystics is that the Hebrew Living Letters were created first out of nothing but God's desire - His divine will. They say, "By use of the letters, the Holy One, Blessed is He, created all the worlds."

On this fifth day of Hanukkah, let the fifth letter of the Hebrew Alef-Bet – *hei* – speak. Behold, the Hebrew Living Letters are the building blocks for all of creation, and they are connected to "let there be light." They are the essence of all light and life.

"In the beginning was the Word, and the Word was with God, and the Word was God" (John 1.1). The Word is made up of letters. *"In the beginning God created alef-tav …" (Genesis 1.1).* The letters – these individual spiritual forces – inherent in Christ were birthed from His essential, intrinsic essence, which was originally included wholly in the Word. The first born of all creation is the very thing that constitutes every living substance. It is the protoplasm of the universe. It is the individual spiritual forces that originally belonged, and still belong, to the nature of Christ. The first born of all creation is the letters of the Word – the Hebrew Living Letters from *alef* to *tav.*

The spiritual realm, where the Almighty dwells, is composed of perfection – pure thoughts and concepts, not needing to be clothed in words and letters. When Yeshua created the Hebrew Living Letters, He ordered spiritual forces of creation through its twenty-two sacred letters before there was another act of creation. The existence of everything created from lions to lemons depends upon the spiritual content with which it was created. By uttering the famous "Let there be…" words, the Word Yeshua created all of what can be classified as Creation.

Like some sort of excellent, exalted scientist, Yeshua spoke the perfect blend of spiritual forces that produces light (Genesis 1.3), produces heaven and all its fullness (Genesis 1.6), produces vegetation yielding seed (Genesis 1.11), and so on ad infinitum. With the words, "Let there be…" creation came into existence in a space-time continuum at that primeval instant. He *"upholds all things by the word of His power" (Hebrews 1.3)*. Everything continues to exist because not an instant goes by without God continuing to say, in effect, "Let there be…" in the sense that the divine will of the original six days remain in force.

Discussion Questions:

1. What was the first born of all creation?

2. Why is language and letters so important?

*****

DAY 6 – Let Your Light Shine!

"The spirit of man is the candle of the LORD, searching all the inward parts of the belly" (Proverbs 20.27 KJV).

There is a ceaseless supply of oil connected to the quintessential verse of Hanukkah: *"Not by might, nor by power, but by My Spirit, says the Lord of Hosts" (Zechariah 4.6).*

Wise virgins take not that "the spirit of man is the lamp of the Lord" (Proverbs 20.27). In this hour, the seven eyes of the Lord, which are the Seven Spirits of God, are looking over your entire earth (Zechariah 4.10). Let Him enlighten your eyes with wisdom and understanding, so your heart can be entirely His: *"For the eyes of the LORD run to and fro throughout the whole earth; therefore, be strong, and let your heart be perfect towards His worship, and understand all His wonders; for the LORD your God will fight for you" (2 Chronicles 16.9 Aramaic).*

Let your light so shine before men that when they see you that they will fall down on their knees in worship saying: "What must I do to be saved?!"

"[14] You are the light of the world. A city that is set on a hill cannot be hidden. [15] Nor do they light a lamp and put it under a basket, but on a lampstand, and it gives light to all who are in the house. [16] Let your light so shine before men, that they may see your good works and glorify your Father in heaven" (Matthew 5.14-16 NKJV).

Discussion Questions:

1. How can you let your light shine?

2. Why do you think that the Seven Spirits of God are called the seven eyes of the Lord?

*****

DAY 7 – All Believers Meeting Together

"The apostles performed many miraculous signs and wonders among the people. And all the believers used to meet together in Solomon's Colonnade" *(Acts 5.12 NIV).*

All the believers met together in Solomon's Colonnade. Did you catch that? This was the ancient practice of the first-century church. I believe that *"all the believers meeting together in Solomon's Colonnade"* is very prophetic for our day, since Yeshua walked in the Temple in Solomon's Colonnade during the Feast of Dedication (John 10.22-23).

God is changing history through a shaking and a rumbling via the full council of the Word of God. We could call it the "Great Quakening." Somehow the seven Feasts of the Lord becoming nine Biblical Bridal Feasts in this Kingdom Day is part of the Great Quakening.

If you want to be wed to the King of Kings, you will want to "do" the Biblical Feasts. The primitive root for "feasts" in 2 Chronicles 8.13 is the same Hebrew word for when Adam intimately knew Eve – *ya'ad.* Biblical Feasts are the vehicles by which those who want to be one with the Messiah meet at His designated times at His designated places to become married.

Yeshua Himself attaches a prophetic significance to the Feast of Dedication – Hanukkah – by telling us that the first Abomination of Desolation (Antichrist) is a prophetic foreshadow of an even greater abomination that confronts believers in these last days.

Please do not minimize that believers did not even have the markers in the calendar to be able to calculate the fulfillment of the Antichrist being revealed until both Purim and Hanukkah were put in place. In addition to the Biblical Feasts of Purim and Hanukkah prophetically portraying the church becoming the Bride of Christ, we will see all the believers be in one accord in Solomon's Colonnade in the end days. They will understand that Jesus did not celebrate His birth – Christmas. He celebrated Hanukkah, which commemorates the overthrow of Christmas – pagan sun god worship.

Please stop and really think about this. Today, most Christians are doing what the first Antichrist did and they are calling it true worship. Could this be the greater abomination that confronts believers in these last days? Instead of one Antichrist sacrificing to "Christmas," what about millions of Christians? Could the beast (spirit of the Antichrist) exist within you and me?

Daniel prophesied about the arch-villain - the infamous Antichrist portrayed in Hanukkah – 300 years before the event took place. On December 25, the Antichrist erected a pagan sun god statue (idol) of God's Brazen Altar and sacrificed a pig to it. This is the same day that most Christians offer up the same pagan sun god deity in their hearts with most not knowing its meaning or origins. You heart is God's Altar where the ultimate battle for purity is being fought.

Those who have ears to hear. Please do not minimize the Antichrist's connection to Hanukkah. Jesus already forewarned us that in the end days a greater abomination than the first Antichrist will take place, and that is saying something. What if the greater abomination is connected to the most abominable practice in His eyes – sun god worship – that drives His Dwelling Presence far from His Sanctuary – you? See Ezekiel chapter 8 verses 6 and 16. Also, refer to http://wp.me/p158HG-Dx and https://www.youtube.com/watch?v=QbEuq3Tz2Q8.

Discussion Questions:

1. Why do you think that the Antichrist is connected to Hanukkah?

2. Why is it important to examine whether Christmas is part of the greater abomination in the end days?

*****

DAY 8 – Ten Virgins Will Greet the Bridegroom and the Bride

"Then the kingdom of heaven will be like ten virgins who took their lamps and went out to greet the bridegroom and the bride" (Matthew 25:1 Aramaic).

Did you know that the parable of the Ten Virgins starts out with all ten virgins taking their lamps to go greet both the Bridegroom and Bride?

Not all versions of the Bible reveal this mystery of both the Bridegroom and the Bride greeting the ten virgins together, but the Aramaic version does. By the way, the Book of Matthew was originally written in Aramaic: *"Then the kingdom of heaven will be like ten virgins who took their lamps and went out to greet the bridegroom and the bride" (Matthew 25.1 Aramaic).*

The ten virgins represent believers in the Messiah. The Bridegroom is Yeshua (Jesus). The Bride (in this case) is the 144,000 Firstfruits who are a spiritually pure bridal company made up of 144,000 sealed Hebrew souls of all tribes of the children of Israel (Revelation 7.4). The 144,000 Virgin Bride *"are pure. They are those who follow the*

Lamb wherever He goes. These were redeemed by Jesus from among men to be the FIRSTFRUITS to God and to the Lamb" (Revelation 14.4 Aramaic). Nita Johnson shares: "John's vision does not necessarily reflect a people who have never known intimacy with a woman or man. Rather, it speaks of a people whom the Spirit of God has so purified by the Spirit of Burning that it has entered into virgin like purity. These saints walk as Jesus walked, having aborted the world, the rule of the flesh, and the devil from their souls. Their souls are as pure as the gold refined seven times over."

The 144,000 Virgin Company are those who will come with the Bridegroom to greet the ten virgins who will either turn out to be wise or foolish in God's eyes.

When you think of the ten virgins with their oil lamps, please consider that the only Biblical Feast that features lamps of oil is Hanukkah. Selah.

> *"[1] Then the kingdom of heaven will be like ten virgins who took their lamps and went out to greet the bridegroom and the bride. [2] Five of them were wise, and five were foolish. [3] And the foolish ones took their lamps, but took no oil with them. [4] But the wise ones took oil in the vessels with their lamps. [5] As the bridegroom was delayed, they all slumbered and slept. [6] And at midnight there was a cry, Behold, the bridegroom is coming; go out to greet him! [7] Then all the virgins got up and prepared their lamps. [8] And the foolish ones said to the wise ones, Give us some of your oil, for our lamps are going out. [9] Then the wise ones answered, saying, Why, there would not be*

enough for us and for you; go to those who sell and buy for yourselves. [10] *And while they went to buy, the bridegroom came; and those who were ready entered with him into the banqueting house, and the door was locked.* [11] *Afterward the other virgins also came and said, Our lord, our lord, open to us.* [12] *But he answered and said to them, Truly I say to you, I do not know you.* [13] *Be alert, therefore, for you do not know the day nor the hour" (Matthew 25,1-13 Aramaic).*

Discussion Questions:

1. Who makes up the 144,000 Virgin Bride Company?

2. How do you think that the wise virgins are connected to the Biblical Feast that features lamps of oil?

*****

6 – MYSTERIES OF ONENESS

DAY 1 – Examine the Heart of a Matter

"Prove me, O LORD, and try me; examine my mind and my heart"
(Psalm 26.2 Aramaic).

In Psalm 26.2, King David is asking for the testing and trying of his innermost parts. When you think about the man said to be after God's own heart, consider that David's feelings and emotions were connected to his innermost parts. As a priest made after the Order of Melchizedek, David knew the Kingdom of God within him needed to be refined in the All-Consuming Fire, so he could come forth as gold (Psalm 110.4; Luke 17.21; Hebrews 12.29; Job 23.10).

It's extremely difficult to see our own blind spots, which in many cases are idols of our own hearts. Therefore, it's crucial to lay all our belief systems and preconceived notions on His Altar before we ask that the Lord tests and tries us. I don't know about you, but I hate to waste a good trial. King David also put it this way: *"[23]Search me, O God, and know my heart: try me, and know my thoughts: [24]And see if there be any wicked way in me, and lead me in the way everlasting" (Psalms 139.23-24 KJV).*

People are continual asking: "If your heart is truly right, is it wrong?" Let's get our mind off a single issue in order to examine the heart of the matter – your heart.

Every single person can say that their heart is right about anything, and I mean anything. How do you think abusers justify what they do? The reality is that we can believe something in our hearts, but it may not be as we believe. *Proverbs 14.12* says: *"There is a way that seems right to a man, but its end is the way of death."* Our hearts are not the arbitrators of truth. God is. That's why David persistently pressed into Him. *"Create in me a clean heart, O God, and renew a steadfast spirit within me" (Psalm 51.10 NKJV).*

Let God Himself test and try the soil of your heart in all matters. There is an answer to the *Jeremiah 17.9* question: *"The heart is deceitful above all things, and desperately wicked: who can know it?"* That answer is our Heavenly Father knows our heart. The one who loves us and wants the best for us.

The problem with carnal, fleshly and worldly things is that we all can be so easily deceived. Therefore, we need to stick to the plumb line of Scripture. Not religiously, but in a life-giving way with a good dose of the Spirit of the

Living God too. I'd like to re-emphasize that to see our own blind spots – like the idols of our hearts – we have to put the matter on God's Altar to burn up any personal desires; then ask the Lord about it. Ask how God see the heart of the matter.

If festivals (like Hanukkah and Christmas) are all about worship; then it is not what we want or think that matters, but what He wants and thinks. Within the context of Scripture, there is great liberty; but mixing pagan things with holy things is a big no-no on His list, which prohibits His Dwelling Presence from residing in you. Please refer to https://www.youtube.com/watch?v=QbEuq3Tz2Q8 and/ or http://wp.me/p158HG-Dx.

Discussion Questions:

1. Why should you have the courage to ask God to try you?

2. What does God think about mixing the holy with the profane?

*****

DAY 2 – Given to You to Know Mysteries

"[11] And Jesus said to them, To you is given to know the mystery of the Kingdom of God, but to outsiders everything has to be explained by parables. [12] For seeing they see, and yet do not perceive; and hearing they hear, and yet do not understand; if they should return, their sin would be forgiven. [13] And he said to them, Go you not understand this parable? How then will you understand all the parables?" (Mark 4.11-13 Aramaic).

"Unto you has been given to know the mystery of the Kingdom of God: but unto them that are without all these things are done in parables" (Mark 4.11 KJV). This passage in Mark chapter 4 goes on to tell us that if we know the Parable of the Sower, we know all parables (Mark 4.13 KJV). We are told plainly in Yeshua's interpretation of the Parable of the Sower that the seed is the Word of God (Luke 8.11), and this seed is sown in our hearts (Mark 4.15). Therefore, a major key to unlocking all mysteries is the Word of God being deposited in the rich, fertile soil of one's heart. We can think of the Word of God being like a decoder ring into the mysteries of God.

The word "mystery" has fascinated me for some time now. There are twenty-one references in Scripture connected to the word "mystery." For example: It has been given to Christ's disciples to know the mysteries of the Kingdom of Heaven and the mysteries of the Kingdom of God (Matthew 13.11; Luke 8.10; Mark 4.11). We are charged to be good stewards of the mysteries of God (1 Corinthians 4.1), and that the wisdom of God is spoken by the Spirit of God among those who are made after the Order of Melchizedek (i.e., among those that are perfect – 1 Corinthians 2.7).

We have the mystery of the Kingdom of Heaven, the mystery of the Kingdom of God, the mystery of the gospel, et cetera. The seed of the Word of God also reveals the Mystery of Iniquity (2 Thessalonians 2.7) and "Mystery, Babylon the Great, the mother of harlots and abominations of the earth" (Revelation 17.5).

There are many dimensions to the Mystery of Iniquity and Mystery Babylon. To keep things as simple as possible, please allow my *Webster's Collegiate Dictionary (10th Edition)* to speak about these profane things through its definition of the word "mystery":

> **mystery** *~noun* : a religious truth that one can know only by revelation and cannot fully understand : a Christian sacrament (1) a secret religious rite believed (as in Eleusian and Mithraic cults) to impart enduring bliss to the initiate (2) a cult devoted to such rites.

Screeeeeeccchhhhhh… Let's stop right there. Seriously?! According to the Word of God a Mithraic cult devoted to Sun God Worship should not be connected to a Christian sacrament; but it was, and still is.

Mithra was one of the favorite sun gods adopted by Rome. Mithra was the Persian version of the original Babylonian sun god Tammuz. The *Catholic Encyclopedia* itself credits Mithra's Winter Festival, as claiming strong responsibility for the December 25th date for Christmas. Mithra's Winter Festival was a birth celebration, which was also called "The Nativity," "The Nativity of the Sun," or "The Nativity of the Unconquered Sun."

The first recorded evidence of "Christmas" taking place on December 25th isn't found until the time of Constantine in 336 A.D. History records that Constantine was a devout worshiper of the sun god *Sol Invictus Mithra* as well as spearheading building the Vatican atop the hill where the Mithra's cult worshiped the sun.

For 300 years, or so, God's people solely celebrated His Biblical Feasts. Know that throughout antiquity, the celebrated birthday of all sun gods was the ancient winter solstice before the Roman shift in time, which was December 25th.

Even though the phrase "Christ's mass" (Christmas) is first found in 1038 A.D. according to the *Catholic Encyclopedia*, I use the term to help people track our modern winter revels with those of the past. Prior to the 11th century, Christmastime was associated with the Winter Solstice, Midwinter, or Winter Revels. For simplicity sake, I say "Christmas" most times instead of the Winter Solstice. Christmas has many Winter Solstice predecessors, but the two most immediate predecessors prior to it being magically Christianized in 379 A.D. are:

[1] Today's CHRISTMAS DAY was originally Mithra's Winter Festival called "The Nativity," which was always celebrated on December 25th – the ancient winter solstice.

[2] Today's CHRISTMAS SEASON was formerly the December celebration of the Saturnalia, which was the worship of the ancient Chaldean god Saturn. Saturn is the image Aaron tried to replicate in fashioning the Golden Calf.

Christmas was originally a secret religious rite for the pagan elite in Rome. The Mithraic Cult was devoted to worshipping the birth day of their sun god on the ancient Winter Solstice. Its origins are in Babylon, specifically Chaldea. Please refer to http://wp.me/p158HG-1t. Its practices include sorcery (lies, control and manipulation), sun god worship, and the land of merchant's status (materialism). Its original icon was a golden calf said to represent the divinity of the ancient Chaldean god Saturn. See http://wp.me/p158HG-2m or https://www.youtube.com/watch?v=INypfLsTaPw.

It has been given to the sons of the Living God to know this Mithraic Cult Mystery. Even though my *Webster's Collegiate Dictionary* says that one definition of "mystery" is a secret rite in the Mithraic Cult said to impart enduring bliss to its participants, ultimately the result is the opposite. Know that roots of Christmas require all its participants to bow down to the pagan sun gods under a tree, which hinders the most supreme eternal bliss for those who worship at Mithra's Table. Refer to https://www.youtube.com/watch?v=fvrVXjd-mm8 or https://santatizing.wordpress.com/2014/12/06/the-roots-of-christmas/.

The Word of God tells us to worship another god is idolatry, which Christmas' connection to the Golden Calf unmistakably illustrates. Not only will idolatry keep us from inheriting the Kingdom of God (Galatians 5.19-20; 1 Corinthians 6.9-10), but it will obviously keep us from being part of the pure and spotless Bride of Christ, which is the epitome of eternal bliss.

> *"30 For we are members of His Body, of His flesh, and of His bones. 31 For this cause shall a man leave his father and mother, and shall be joined unto his wife, and they two shall be one flesh. 32 This is a great mystery: but I speak concerning Christ and the church" (Ephesians 5.30-32 KJV).*

Discussion Questions:

1. Will God join Himself to an idol?

2. What are some facets of the great mystery of Christ and the church?

*****

DAY 3 – Tethering To Eternity

"[9] Know ye not that the unrighteous shall not inherit the Kingdom of God? Be not deceived: neither fornicators, nor idolaters, nor adulterers, nor effeminate, nor abusers of themselves with mankind, [10] nor thieves, nor covetous, nor drunkards, nor revilers, nor extortioners, shall inherit the Kingdom of God. [15] Know ye not that your bodies are the members of Christ? Shall I then take the members of Christ, and make them the members of a harlot? God forbid. [16] What! Know ye not that he which is joined to a harlot is one body? For two, saith He, shall be one flesh. [17] But he that is joined unto the Lord is one spirit"
(1 Corinthians 6.9-10, 15-17 KJV).

Many Christians believe that they are connecting to the true Messiah Yeshua (Jesus Christ) during Christmas, but history and Scripture reveals a different eternal reality.

First, always remember that Yeshua celebrated Hanukkah, not Christmas. See John 10.22-23. Yeshua has shown us the way, the truth and the life for every Winter One-der-land season. More than that, Yeshua has shown us the eternal reality of the One New Man in Christ (Messiah), which is Metatron in its fullness.

It is not a coincidence that the Messiah in His fullness is called Metatron. The completely mature head of Yeshua connected to the completely mature members of His Body embodies many things. Let's simply focus on Metatron being the keeper of time. Metatron Messiah is the keeper of space-time… three-dimensional space and the fourth dimension of time.

In contrast, the world currently has a false Metatron figure called Metatron Mithra. The counterfeit Metatron Mithra is said to be the god of agriculture and time too. Metatron Mithra embodies the false control of space-time. Stick with me, as we paint a picture of Christmas being part of the illusion of space-time that's connects its adherents to religious Babylon and Saturn (i.e., Satan – the prince of this world).

For simplicity sake, we are going to continue to contrast Metatron Messiah with Metatron Mithra. Let's unlock the Metatron Mithra piece first. The demonic control of space-time is literally connected to Metatron Mithra. If you and I want to manifest resurrection life and become just like Jesus – connected to the fullness of the heavenly One New Man in the Messiah – you will have to pass the litmus test for purification at His Gateway of Awe in His Winter One-der-land.

For over 8 years now, I have repeatedly revealed that there is two immediate predecessors for Christmas before Rome officially assimilated it into its official church calendar in the fourth century:

[1] CHRISTMAS DAY's immediate predecessor was Mithra's Winter Festival. The *Catholic Encyclopedia* admits that the Nativity of the Unconquered Sun (another name for Mithra's

Winter Festival) has strong claim on the responsibility of our December 25th date. Did you catch that? The worship of Metatron Mithra is literally the root of Christmas Day. This is a primary anchor for tethering God's people to the illusion of the corrupted reality of space-time.

[2] CHRISTMAS SEASON's immediate predecessor was the ancient Yuletide Season called the Saturnalia. The Saturnalia took carnal indulgences to an extreme. Nine months later, all the illegitimate children born from the occasion, were called Saturnalians. When the faithful heathens worshiped Saturn, no fleshly indulgence was too extreme; including, adultery, fornication, reveling, idolatry, murder, etc. You get the idea. The worship of Saturn during the winter solstice season basically fills out the bill for the works of the flesh that we are not supposed to do, if believers want to inherit the Kingdom of God (1 Corinthians 6.10-11; Galatians 5.19-21).

When the High Priest Aaron fabricated a golden calf to depict God, he was looking back to Egypt to the Apis bull. This golden calf was said to represent the divinity of the ancient Chaldean (Babylonian) god – Saturn. Which brings us to our topic at hand – being tethered in an unholy way to space-time. The worship of Saturn has been anciently connected to the Black Cube. The Black Cube is the antithesis of the Golden Cube of the New Jerusalem. The Black Cube literally represents the god of this world's control of time and space

Amazing as it may seem, Christmas Day and the Christmas Season both act as tethers to an ungodly false reality. It is time to take the red pill or the blue. Are you going to be hot for Metatron Messiah and his glorious eternal reality? Or are you going to be cold, choosing Metatron Mithra instead? It's one of the ultimate tests of a person's heart. God is so good. We each get to choose.

Choose this day the Golden Cube or the Black Cube. Choose this day the true Messiah Metatron Yeshua, or the False Messiah Metatron Mithra.

Discussion Questions:

1. What other connections can you come up with between the true Messiah Metatron Yeshua and the False Messiah Metatron Mithra?

2. Why does God allow the false Metatron Mithra to control a false illusion of space-time?

*****

DAY 4 – Four Abominations Determine Degree of Four Faces of God

"Son of man, do you see what they are doing … things that will drive Me far from My Sanctuary?" (Ezekiel 8.6 KJV).

Do you really want to see what drives God from His Dwelling Place – you? Do you want God to simply visit you? Or do you want to have God dwell with you and you dwell with God?

The four idolatrous practices listed in Ezekiel 8.3-5, 9-12, 14, 16 originate in Babylon, and the Bible says that they are detestable to God. All four of these idolatrous practices have to do with pure worship. The fourth and most detestable in God's eyes maps to our modern-day Christmas: *"So He brought me into the inner court of the LORD's house; and there, at the door of the Temple of the LORD, between the porch and the altar, were about twenty-five men with their backs toward the temple of the LORD and their faces toward the east, and they were worshiping the sun toward the east" (Ezekiel 8.16 NKJV).* These twenty-five or so men knew and loved the Lord; yet they still grievously bowed down to worship the sun, whether they acknowledged the fact or not.

"About 25"… How many times do you see an approximation in Scripture? It's very unusual. "About 25" is a Bible Code that's communicating it's all "about 25." It's about the 25th. It's about the 25th of December. Throughout antiquity, all sun gods across all cultures celebrated the sun gods' birthday on the ancient winter solstice – December 25th – before the Roman shift in time. Recall that Christmas Day's immediate predecessor was Mithra's Winter Festival, which has strong claim on the Christian Church's December 25th date for Christmas. Our modern-day Christmas Season's immediate predecessor is the Roman Saturnalia, which literally link Christmas to the Gold Calf that Aaron made.

The pagans in the fourth century recognized their own solar cults in the church's adoption of the Nativity of the Unconquered Sun (Mithra's Winter Festival). They recognized the church's assimilation of their pagan practices in orienting cathedrals to the east, worshiping on "sun day," and celebrating the birth of the sun god deity at the Winter Solstice. Pagans not only recognized all these Constantine Compromises, they also went on worshiping in their pagan way. History records that it had become common practice in the fifth century for worshipers entering St. Peter's Basilica in Rome to turn at the door, put their backs to the altar, and bow down to worship the rising sun.

Yeshua is telling us that Christmas is a golden calf, which means it's idolatry in His eyes. We have each been given the responsibility to prepare a place for Him: " [2] *When He appears, we shall be like Him; for we shall see Him as He is.* [3]

Everyone who has this hope in Him purifies himself, just as He is pure" (1 John 3.2-3).

His shekinah glory cannot dwell where there is idolatry; therefore, His dwelling presence cannot, and will not, coexist with this golden calf we call Christmas. Idolatry is a crux that determines whether His shekinah glory will merely visit His people or dwell among them. It is essential to lay down all idolatry to take on your cherubic nature, like Enoch did. If it's your heart-of-hearts to participate in the fullness of God's glorious Melchizedek and Bridal Companies, you must pass through this fire.

The four abominations in Ezekiel 8 that drive God's Dwelling Presence far from His sanctuary map to the four faces of God. We can also call them the four faces of Melchizedek. To the degree that we compromise with the four abominations is the degree that we won't operate in the fullness of the Cherubim Classification of the Order of Melchizedek.

We have seen that Christmas Day is rooted in the sun god worship of Mithra (Mithraism). It is not a coincidence that the centerpiece of every Mithraeum was a sculpture of Mithra killing a sacred bull. The worship of Mithra compromises the face of the ox – the Father – which the Cherubim (Corporate Order of Melchizedek) is supposed to operate in.

The Pattern Son – Yeshua – descended and ascended to take captivity captive. Each Melchizedek Priest will have to bring this Christmas worship issue before the Lord when they descend into the throne within; then once rectified, we ascend to re-establish the fullness of the Face of the Ox (Father God) to be made whole.

Christmas is the ultimate crux for God's Dwelling Presence that will determine if you will take on your cherubic nature, or not. And you get to choose. In the *Third Book of Enoch*, we are told that the splendor of His shekinah was on earth until the time of the generation of Enosh when they erected idols in every quarter of the world and brought down THE SUN, the moon, planets and constellations and placed them before their idols.

We know that the manifest dwelling presence of God – His Shekinah – left the Christian Church when pagan holidays were assimilated into it. Historical proof is seen in the departure of daily miracles from among them. Scriptural proof is spelled out in Ezekiel 8-11. For more on this subject, please check out this video => https://www.youtube.com/watch?v=QbEuq3Tz2Q8.

Discussion Questions:

1. Can you tell us why Christmas compromises the Face of the Ox, i.e., Father God? (See the book *SANTA-TIZING: What's wrong with Christmas and how to clean it up* => https://www.amazon.com/SANTA-TIZING-Whats-wrong-Christmas-clean/dp/1607911159 and the *MEL GEL Study*

Guide =>
https://www.amazon.com/dp/0578188538/.)

2. Why is sun god worship (Christmas) the most detestable thing in God's eyes that drives Him from His sanctuary – you and me? (See Ezekiel 8.6,16)

*****

DAY 5 – Compromising the Face of the Ox

"'But the hour is coming, and now is, when the true worshipers will worship the Father in spirit and truth; for the Father is seeking such to worship Him" (John 4.23 NKJV).

When man (i.e., Israel) sinned, the face of the ox was replaced with the cherub: *"And every one had four faces: the first face was the face of the cherub, and the second face was the face of a man, and the third face of a lion, and the fourth face of an eagle" (Ezekiel 10.14 KJV).* This is why the priest must go back up. Each Melchizedek Priest must ascend to re-establish the Face of the Ox in their own life. They must connect to their incredible Heavenly Father to be made whole again.

But there is another astounding dimension to the face of the ox being replaced by the cherubim. Ezekiel chapter 10 tells us that the four faces in Ezekiel 1 – lion, ox, eagle and man – are the same faces that are in Ezekiel 10 – lion, cherub, eagle and man: *"And the likeness of their faces was the same faces which I saw by the river Chebar, their appearances and themselves" (Ezekiel 10.22 KJV).* What this can mean is that the Cherubim, which is a Corporate Order of Melchizedek, is the same as the face of the ox.

The ox is the face of the Father, which is why *Mystic Mentoring (in Christ) Group Ascensions* set their focus on the Father (John 5.30; Romans 12.2). A group becomes the Cherubim Classification of the Order of Melchizedek when they focus on the perfect heart of the Father, or in other words, the perfect will of the Father. This is the reason Mystic Mentoring Group Ascensions focus on the Father before, during and even after our corporate ascensions.

Yesterday, we discussed the how the four abominations in Ezekiel chapter 8, which drive God's Dwelling Presence from His sanctuary map to the four faces of God (Melchizedek). To the degree that we compromise with the four abominations is the degree that we don't operate in the fullness of the Cherubim.

Christmas Day is rooted in the sun god worship of Mithra (Mithraism). It's not a coincidence that the centerpiece of every Mithraeum was a sculpture of Mithra killing a sacred bull. The Worship of Mithra compromises the Face of the Ox – the Face of the Father – which the Cherubim Classification of the Order of Melchizedek is supposed to operate in.

Not only does Christmas compromise the Face of the Ox (the Father), but due to the Christmas Season's root being Saturn worship, people are connecting to the Black Cube of Saturn instead of the Crystal-Clear Golden Cube of the New Jerusalem.

Either of these connections will short-circuit anyone taking on the fullness of their cherubic nature, which is becoming divine just like Yeshua (Genesis 1.26-27). Even more grave than tethering a person to the demonic control of space-time, think about how this must grieve our Heavenly Father's heart. *"But the hour is coming, and now is, when the true worshipers will worship the Father in spirit and truth; for the Father is seeking such to worship Him" (John 4.23 NKJV).*

Discussion Questions:

1. Why do the priests of the Order of Melchizedek have to ascend?

2. What two connections associated with Christmas tether you to the demonic control of space-time?

*****

DAY 6 – New Jerusalem Connection to the Messiah

"These are those who were not defiled with women, for they are pure. These are those who follow the Lamb wherever He goes. These were redeemed by Jesus from among men to be the first fruits to God and to the Lamb" (Revelation 14.4 Aramaic).

The 144,000 Virgin Bride is the *"first fruits unto God and to the Lamb … who follow the Lamb wherever He goes" (Revelation 14.4).* The perfect resurrection of the Messiah's Body will inaugurate the Age of the Bride of Christ… the Age of the New Jerusalem… the Age of the Perfect One New Man in the Messiah – Metatron. Think of Metatron being the literal fullness of the Messiah.

Who will initially participate in the perfect resurrection of the Messiah's Body? The First Fruits Bridal Company who will inherit the Kingdom of God, because they have chosen to die to this world completely laying down all works of the flesh (Galatians 5.19-21).

The first Antichrist (Antiochus Epiphanes IV) celebrated Christmas, before it was called "Christmas." He placed a Greek sun god on God's Altar; and then, sacrificed a pig on it. Jesus celebrated the antithesis. Scripture reveals that Yeshua celebrated the Feast of Dedication (Hanukkah). It's recorded in John 10.22-23. Jesus celebrated the overthrow of the defilement of Christmas on God's Altar (i.e., our hearts).

Recall that Christmas had the two immediate predecessors prior to being assimilated into the church in the fourth century:

[1] CHRISTMAS DAY was a worship-filled activity centered around Mithra's Winter Festival (Sol Invictus Mithra) on the ancient winter solstice – December 25th. Mithra was a Persian sun god adopted by the Roman Legion; but more importantly, we should note that the false fullness of the Messiah figure is called Metatron Mithra.

[2] CHRISTMAS SEASON was a wild party called the Roman Saturnalia, which was connected to the most ancient Yuletide Season. Not only was the Saturnalia a season of extreme carnal excess, it also featured the worship of Saturn. When Aaron tried to depict the divinity of the Most High God as a golden calf, he looked back to Egypt to the calf that represented the divinity of the ancient Chaldean (Babylonian) god – Saturn – which also anciently connects to the Black Cube that endeavors to control space-time.

It is not a coincidence that the true Messiah in His fullness (completely mature Head of Yeshua with His completely mature Body) is called Metatron, and Metatron is the keeper of space-time.

Believers will either choose to come out of Babylon and lay down Christmas to become a precious part of His Pure and Spotless Bride or not. If you choose to keep Christmas, know that you are choosing to connect with a false Messiah – Mithra – as well as choosing to connect to the Black Cube, which symbolizes the satanic control of space-time. Please note: If you want to be transfigured, like Enoch, and become connect to the Mature Head of Messiah Metatron Yeshua as part of His Mature Body, you will have to untether from all mixture and the satanic control structure.

Remember that Yeshua (Jesus) celebrated Hanukkah while the Antichrist in the Hanukkah story essentially celebrated Christmas. The Antichrist (Antiochus Epiphanes IV) first removed the rightful High Priest; then outlawed God's people ability to keep their time holy through outlawing Biblical celebrations and making them punishable by death. Today, realize that the spirit of the Antichrist has to first dethrone the rightful High Priest after the Order of Melchizedek – Jesus Christ – from a certain place in your heart in order to get you to agree and to defend the worship of a beguiling Messianic image of Mithra on December 25th. It doesn't matter if the façade of Jesus' birth is there. It's an elaborate and emotionally captivating ruse to steal God's most precious possession – the Bride of the Messiah. Know that God is using all of this too. Only the most ardent, devout, and self-sacrificial will follow through in truly examining the lamb of Christmas, which typically funnels God's people's most generous worship of the year. What if the Lord is truly asking all of us to sacrifice all for Jesus?

When believers choose to connect to the true Messiah through their heart, which is demonstrated in their actions, many things in this world grow strangely dim, including the tinsel of Christmas. Know that the Pure and Spotless Bride of Christ, who is one with her Beloved Bridegroom Yeshua is the essence of the New Jerusalem. Only the most devout ones will fully connect to Messiah Yeshua Metatron and His crystal-clear golden cube of the New Jerusalem.

Choose this day the Golden Cube or the Black Cube. Choose this day the True Messiah Metatron Yeshua or the False Messiah Metatron Mithra. *"I call heaven and earth to bear witness against you this day, that I have set before you life and death, blessings and curses; therefore choose life, that both you and your descendants may live" (Deuteronomy 30.19 Aramaic).*

Discussion Questions:

1. Why does God allow such intense trials and testings, which the battle over Christmas is simply one humongous test?

2. Why is the choosing between the Golden Cube of the New Jerusalem and the Black Cube of Saturn (Satan) so crucial?

*****

DAY 7 – 144000 and the Giant Golden Cube

"[16] And the city was laid foursquare, the length the same as the breadth; and he measured the city with the reed, twelve furlongs, twelve thousand paces. And the length and breadth and the height were equal. [17] And he measured the wall thereof, a hundred and forty and four cubits, according to the measure of a man, that is, of the angel. [18] And the wall was constructed of jasper; and the city itself was pure gold, resembling clear glass" (Revelation 21.16-18 Aramaic).

Early Christians imagined the Kingdom of God as the heavenly city – the New Jerusalem – which we are told is the Bride of the Lamb in Revelation 21. It also reveals that the New Jerusalem is a giant golden cube.

> *"[1] Now I saw a new heaven and a new earth, for the first heaven and the first earth had passed away. Also there was no more sea. [2] Then I, John, saw the holy city, New Jerusalem, coming down out of heaven from God, prepared as a bride adorned for her husband. [7] He who overcomes shall inherit all things, and I will be his God and he shall be My son. [8] But the cowardly, unbelieving, abominable, murderers, sexually immoral, sorcerers, idolaters, and all liars shall have their part in the lake of fire and brimstone, which is the second death. [9] Then one of the seven angels who had the seven bowls filled with the seven last plagues came to me and talked with me, saying, 'Come, I will show you the bride, the Lamb's wife.'*

> [10] *And he carried me away in the Spirit to a great and high mountain, and showed me the great city, the holy Jerusalem, descending out of heaven from God,* [11] *having the glory of God. Her light was like a most precious stone, like a jasper stone, clear as crystal.* [16] *The city is laid out as a square; its length is as great as its breadth. And he measured the city with the reed: twelve thousand furlongs.* ITS LENGTH, BREADTH, AND HEIGHT ARE EQUAL. [17] *Then he measured its walls: one hundred and forty-four cubits, according to the measure of a man, that is of an angel.* [18] *The construction of its wall was of jasper; and the city was* PURE GOLD, *like clear glass" (Revelation 21.1-2, 7-10, 16-18 NKJV).*

In sacred geometry, a cube represents the earth. The physical realm, in which we live, is connected to the spiritual realm, which is made up of geometric shapes and patterns. The Order of Melchizedek is called to restore all things. Sacred geometry is simply one of those things. Nancy Coen teaches that the word "wicked" means a slight twisting, like a wick, of a righteous real. We simply must find the "righteous real" and untwist it. The Golden Cube is the "righteous real" or redemption of the Black Cube; and Metatron Messiah Yeshua is the true guardian or holder of the keys to the universe(s) and everything that reside with them. Everything that exists does so, because of Sacred Geometry. The basis of all sacred geometry is the five Platonic solids. The five Platonic solids (shapes) are crucial, because they form the building blocks for all organic life.

Consider that all the Platonic solids are contained within Metatron's Cube. Allow me to me explain. The thirteen circles of Metatron's Cube are the fundamental blueprint of all atomic structure. From the matrix of the 13 spheres, all five Platonic solids can be created, which are the basic geometries of life in all levels of reality. The 13-sphere configuration of Metatron's Cube is a cipher for the restoration of all things. To become tethered to one dimension of Metatron's Cube is to limit you from operating in the unlimited realm. That's what being tethered to the Black Cube and the false Metatron Mithra does. It limits you when eternity has been put in your heart (Ecclesiastes 3.11). It limits you from operating in the fullness of the image you were create – divine (Genesis 1.26-27). It limits you, because you are connecting to a false reality instead of the eternal one. It limits you, because you are in agreement with idolatry and have bought into a lie. Please refer to https://santatizing.wordpress.com/2014/12/06/the-roots-of-christmas/ and https://www.youtube.com/watch?v=fvrVXjd-mm8.

It's very significant that Revelation chapter 21 basically re-emphasizes verse 8 in the last verse of the chapter - verse 27. Notice that *"all liars"* and *"lies"* are mentioned specifically in both places:

- *"But for the fearful and the unbelieving and the sinful and the abominable and murderers and those who commit adultery and magicians and idolaters and all liars, their portion shall be in the lake that burns with fire and brimstone, which is the second death" (Revelation 21.8 Aramaic).*

- *"And there shall not enter into it anything which defiles nor he who works abominations and lies; only those shall enter whose names are written in the Lamb's book of life" (Revelation 21.27 Aramaic).*

I love that the New Jerusalem has no temple, because the Lord Almighty and the Lamb are the temple of it (Revelation 21.22) We are also told that the glory and the honor of the people are brought into the holy city, New Jerusalem (Revelation 21.26).

This giant gold New Jerusalem cube represents the reality of a Kingdom fit for the King of kings of kings where He will dwell with His Queen. Never forget that God's most valuable possession – His Bride is in the midst of God's Kingdom with Him. They are literally one. Therefore, when we ask: Where is the 144,000 Firstfruits in all this? We know that the 144,000 are in the light in the Lamb in the midst of the heavenly city, because they are one with Him. *"The city has no need of the sun, neither of the moon, to shine in it, for the glory of God brightens it and the Lamb is the lamp of it" (Revelation 21.23 Aramaic).*

Discussion Questions:

1. What does the Golden Cube of the New Jerusalem make you think of?

2. How does a person's connection to Christmas, Metatron Mithra and the Black Cube limit them?

*****

DAY 8 – Wedding Supper of the Lamb

"[7] Let us be glad and rejoice and give glory to Him, for the time of the marriage feast of the Lamb has come, and His Bride has made herself ready. [8] And it was given to her that she should be arrayed in fine pure linen, clean and white; for fine linen is the righteousness of saints. [9] And he said to me, Write, Blessed are those who are invited to the wedding feast of the Lamb" (Revelation 19.7-9 Aramaic).

Have you ever thought about the consummation of the ages – the Marriage Supper of the Lamb? Yeshua the Bridegroom and His Beloved Bride married as one. Imagine them feasting together.

All Biblical Feasts are important bridal markers and part of His Eternal Word. The eternal priesthood of the Order of Melchizedek will totally understand and embody these realities.

Recall that the fall and spring feasts in Scripture are rehearsals for Jesus' first and second coming, respectively. Also, recall that the winter feasts in the Bible are important too, because they are a picture of Hs church (i.e., believers) becoming the Bride of Christ. It's vitally important to remember that the primitive root to the word "feasts" in 2 Chronicles 8.13 is the Hebrew word *ya'ad. Ya'ad* is the term used for when Adam intimately know Eve. This primitive *ya-ad* root implies that the Lord is summoning His people to meet Him at His stated time, and He is directing us into a certain position for the purpose of engaging us in marriage. The question that we need to answer is: If we don't celebrate the Lord at His appointed feasts, can we still marry Him?

Let's focus a little more on the two winter feasts portraying the church's journey to become Christ's Bride. Hanukkah shows us a small ragtag group overcoming odds to overthrow the Antichrist of their day while Purim displays the rightful queen standing against the annihilation of her people – God's people – for such a time as this.

These Winter Biblical Feasts illustrate that becoming part of God's pure and spotless Bride doesn't just automatically happen. The parable of the ten virgins in Matthew 25 reveals that the gospel of the kingdom of heaven can be pictured as five wise virgins and five foolish ones. Please understand that these "virgins" are all believers in the Lord Jesus Christ crucified, buried and risen.

The foolish virgins had the door shut on them, as the wise virgins went into the marriage supper of the Lamb, because they had made themselves ready (Matthew 25.10-12). The voice of many waters in Revelation 19 speaks about the Bride making herself ready: *"[6]And I heard as it were the voice of a great multitude, and as the voice of many waters, and as the voice of mighty thunderings, saying, 'Alleluia! For the Lord God Omnipotent reigns! [7]Let us be glad and rejoice and give Him glory, for the marriage of the Lamb has come, and His wife has made herself ready.' [8]And to her it was granted to be arrayed in fine, linen, clean and bright, for the fine linen is the righteous acts of the saints. [9]Then He said to me, 'Write: Blessed are those who are called to the Marriage Supper of the Lamb!' And he said to me, 'These are the true sayings of God'" (Revelation 19.6-9 NKJV).*

Notice that the essence of the clothing that makes the Lamb's wife ready for the Marriage Supper of the Lamb "is the righteous acts of the saints." It's righteousness. The root meaning behind the Hebrew word for "righteousness" tells us that righteous is a State of Being. All truly righteous acts are simply an outflow of who we true are when we are one with Messiah Yeshua. Know that the Messiah's Bride will resonate at the same frequency as her Beloved Bridegroom. Those things in our lives that are not plumb with God's measuring line of righteousness (according to His Word) will cause us to resonate at a lower frequency than a pure and spotless one.

Notice that another parable shows us that clothing is the determining factor for being included in the king's wedding banquet. An inappropriately dressed friend gets thrown out of the king's wedding banquet due to this fact: *"[2] The kingdom of heaven is like a king who gave a wedding banquet for his son… [11] But when the king came in to view the guests, he looked intently at a man there who had on no wedding garment. [12] And he said, Friend, how did you come here without outing on the [appropriate] wedding garment? And he was speechless (muzzled, gagged). [13] Then the king said to the attendants, Tie him hand and foot, and throw him into the darkness outside; there will be weeping and grinding of teeth. [14] For many are called (invited and summoned), but few are chosen" (Matthew 22.2,11-14 Amplified).*

Notice that the king calls this wedding guest "friend," which means he is a believer. For more on this subject, please refer to https://santatizing.wordpress.com/2012/12/31/here-comes-the-bride-part-3/.

The Marriage Supper of the Lamb is the twelfth and final stage of a Hebrew Wedding. It's for all guests invited by the Father of the Bride who are appropriately dressed. Many are called, but few do what is required in order to be part of this festive chosen group.

Discussion Questions:

1. How does the Bride of Christ make herself ready?

2. Who will be at the Wedding Supper of the Lamb?

*****

7 – MYSTERIES OF THE STOREHOUSE OF SNOW

DAY 1 – Choose This Day: Wise Virgins and Foolish Virgins

"Behold, I come quickly; and My reward is with Me,
to give every man according to his work" (Revelation 22.12 KJV).

"Choose this day" is echoing throughout the multiverse. Each of our choices has a consequence that is revealed by our actions. All of us will be known for our fruits: *"Either produce like a good tree with good fruits, or produce like a bad tree with bad fruits; for a tree is known by its fruits" (Matthew 12.33 Aramaic).*

"Even a child is known by his doings, whether his work be pure, and whether it be right" (Proverbs 20.11 NIV). Am I the only one who gets the reverential fear of the Lord when I read Revelation 22.12? *"And, behold I come quickly; and My reward is*

with Me, to give every man according to his work" (Revelation 22.12 KJV).

True believers in Yeshua Ha Machiach (Jesus Christ) have a one-der-ful choice to make in His Winter One-der-land. Christmas and Hanukkah started the same day in 2016 – the evening of December 24, 2016. Each and every one of us will chose in our hearts and by our actions one or the other. By the way, no mixture is allowed for bridal hearts. We will either choose to do what Yeshua did (John 10.22-23), or we will choose what the Antichrist did. Please refer to https://santatizing.wordpress.com/2015/12/02/yeshua-celebrated-hanukkah-not-christmas/and https://www.youtube.com/watch?v=fvrVXjd-mm8.

His Gateway of Awe always has a special grace to cross over. Choose this day. Choose this day the eternal or the temporal => https://santatizing.wordpress.com/2016/12/16/christmas-tether-to-space-time/. We are in a crossover place to choose to party with the King of Kings, as He did while He was on earth, or party with the world while possibly believing otherwise. For more information, check out => http://wp.me/p158HG-kH and http://wp.me/p158HG-DF.

Wise virgins choose to party with the King of Kings, which will fill their lamps with oil to overflowing. Foolish virgins will choose to party with the world while believing that they are doing it all for Jesus. Did you know that the people that partied with the Golden Calf said and did that exact same thing? See http://wp.me/p158HG-kH. At the same time Aaron made an altar to God's specifications, took the people's gold and made a golden idol, Moses received the nation's *ketubah* (i.e., marriage contract), which contained the Ten Commandments.

Too much is at stake – His Pure and Spotless Bride. Won't you truly examine the lamb that you sacrifice as yearly worship to the King? Please refer to http://wp.me/p158HG-rV.

Choose this day the Golden Calf of Christmas or the Marriage Contract of the Bridegroom => https://santatizing.wordpress.com/2016/12/17/choose-this-day-the-golden-calf-or-his-marriage-contract/.

The time is short than you think. Choose this day wise and foolish virgins, for behold, He comes quickly.

Discussion Questions:

1. What are the fruits of Hanukkah and Christmas? Please examine both good and bad and realize a good tree does not produce bad fruit (Matthew 3.10).

2. Why should you choose to party with the King of Kings, as He did and does?

*****

DAY 2 – Journey to Become His Bride: History of Hanukkah – Part I

"[12] And because iniquity shall abound, the love of many shall wax cold. [13] But he that shall endure into the end, the same shall be saved. [14] And this gospel of the kingdom shall be preached in all the world for a witness unto all nations; and then shall the end come. [15] When ye therefore shall see the abomination of desolation, spoken of by Daniel the prophet, stand in the holy place, (whoso readeth, let him understand,) … [21] For then shall be great tribulation, such as was not since the beginning of the world to this time, no, nor ever will be. [22] And except those days should be shortened, there should no flesh be saved: but for the elect's sake those days shall be shortened" (Matthew 24.12-15, 21-22 KJV).

During Hanukkah, Yeshua (Jesus) celebrated the overthrow of Christmas on God's Altar. Please refer to http://wp.me/p158HG-Gn and http://wp.me/p158HG-GN.

At the risk of death, Yeshua went up to Jerusalem to meet with believers, celebrate Hanukkah, and perform the most essential miracle that proved that he is the Messiah. Please see http://wp.me/p158HG-H1. When we combine the overthrow of Christmas on God's Altar (i.e., the love of Christmas in a person's heart) with Yeshua healing a man born blind, we receive a vital connectedness key for the One New Man in the Messiah and His Bride. Therefore, we need to dive into what the Feast of Dedication (Hanukkah) is all about. The history of Hanukkah reveals the prophetic significance to what Yeshua did and what the Messiah's Bride will have to do to join Him.

The year was 168 B.C. The city was Jerusalem. The desecration of God's Altar was perpetrated on Jupiter's Winter Festival, which was the 15th of Kislev, which happened to coincide with the 25th of December that year. Some people say it was a statue of Zeus put on God's Altar. Some say it was Jupiter. In a sense, it really doesn't matter, because both of them were Greek sun gods. Never forget that the predecessor for Christmas Day worship is pagan sun god worship.

When the Greeks under Antiochus Epiphanes IV set up the abomination of desolation in 168 B.C., as foretold in the Book of Daniel, all evening and morning sacrifices ceased (Daniel 11.31, Daniel 12.11). Yeshua tells us that the first abomination of desolation was a prophetic foreshadow of an even greater abomination that confronts believers in the last days (Matthew 24.11, 21). Please refer to http://wp.me/p158HG-Gi and http://wp.me/p158HG-GN.

Exactly three years to the day after Jupiter's statue was put on God's Altar and a pig was sacrificed to him, the Maccabees rejoiced as they began the re-dedication of God's Altar, and thus God's Temple, in Jerusalem. This was the first feast of Hanukkah. By the way, "Hanukkah" means dedication. In the both apocrypha books of the Maccabees, the myth of the eight-day miraculous supply of oil has been left out. It's all about the Altar (i.e., the heart).

Let's dive a little deeper into the history of the first Hanukkah. Before the crucifixion of Jesus Christ, the Jewish people experienced a man and a world-impacting movement that strove to change God's times and law. The Seleucid General Antiochus Epiphanes IV history infamously classifies him as an Antichrist. The world-impacting movement he promoted was Hellenism. When Greek culture mixed with the culture of the Middle East, it created a hybrid called Hellenism. Antiochus' goal was to make people one in the image that he chose, after all he had taken on the title "Epiphanes," which means God manifest.

Antiochus Epiphanes IV was rightly portrayed an Antichrist. Josephus tells us that he polluted the altar of God by offering up swine on it, knowing that this was against the Law of Moses. Antiochus forced God's people to bow before his pagan sun god under penalty of death. Many innocent people were massacred and the survivors were heavily taxed. The *Book of Maccabees* calls this period a "reign of terror." In keep with Daniel 7.25, Antiochus IV took four deliberate steps between 169 and 167 BC to forcibly "hellenize" the people of The Book:

[1] First to be dealt with was the seat of power in Judea – the High Priest. Antiochus removed

the sitting High Priest whose name meant "righteous peace," and replaced him with a Jew who would do man's bidding. By the way, from this point on, the high priesthood in Israel largely became a corrupt institution.

[2] Secondly, Antiochus tried to dissolve the Biblical Calendar. He felt that these people were time obsessed in trying to keep their time holy. Antiochus felt if he destroyed these people's sense of time, he could destroy their ability to practice their religion. Therefore, Antiochus IV forbid the observance of the seventh day Sabbath that set the people's weeks, the new moon celebrations that set their months, and festivals that set their years. These Biblical marks of time were symbols of man's obligation to instill holiness into time. These were all appointed meeting places in time between God and man.

[3] Antiochus forbade the studying of the Word of God (Torah, which is the first five books of the Bible) and keeping kosher (respecting the sanctity of life). Torah scrolls were publicly burnt, as pigs were sacrificed over them to defile them. Antiochus even forced the High Priest to institute swine sacrifices in God's Temple in Jerusalem as well as permitting worship of various Greek gods

(I Maccabees 1.41-64).

[4] Lastly, Antiochus forbade circumcision. To Jews, this was their physical sign of their covenant of faith with God (i.e., Abrahamic Covenant) that demonstrates that the physical and spiritual are intertwined. Circumcision was the body's mark to allegiance to God's covenant that spoke of being a servant, not a master. To the Greeks, circumcision was seen as mutilation, because they worshiped the perfection of the human body and its sensuality.

When the Abomination of Desolation was set up in Jerusalem, a general directive was sent to Antiochus' entire kingdom that all people must relinquish their own customs and religions to conform to the Greek culture and creed; but another directive was expressively sent to Judea, which demanded that the sacrificial service cease in Jerusalem's Temple. In its place, altars and temple should be set up everywhere for idol-worship where unclean animals were to be sacrificed. As if that was not enough, Antiochus commanded that the Holy Temple be desecrated and converted into a pagan temple. This is when the statue of Jupiter/Zeus was erected upon the Altar on the 15th of Kislev 168 B.C. (I Maccabees 1.54). It is also when all things that these Biblical people considered holy was prohibited: observance of Sabbath, Rosh Chodesh (New Moon), Biblical festivals, dietary laws, covenant of circumcision, laws of family purity, and even the use of God's name. Then beginning on the 25th of this month, hogs were offered upon the sun god's altar (I Maccabees 1.59).

Most people complied with the pagan king's barbarous order, but many chose death above desecrating the Name. In those troubled times, Mattisyahu the Hasmonean, the son of Yochanan (John) a previous high priest, left Jerusalem where persecution was strongest. He and his family settled in a Judean village near Jerusalem called Modin.

One day the king's forces appeared in Modin and demanded that the town sacrifice in the pagan fashion. They chose the most respected man in town. Mattisyahu, to comply (I Maccabees 2.17-18). Bribery was the door for many to pagan conversion. If Mattisyahu would simply sacrifice a pig and eat it, he and his sons would be considered the king's friends'. Which was an official title that carried many privileges including social and material advantages.

As Mattisyahu was defiantly refusing the pagan honor, a turncoat Jew neared the pagan altar to offer the sacrifice (I Maccabees 2.19-24). Mattisyahu was filled with righteous indignation at this blatant desecration of "The Name." In the tradition of Phineas, Mattisyahu grabbed a sword and killed the Jewish traitor on the altar along with the messenger of the pagan king (I Maccabees 2.24-26). After tearing down the altar, Mattisyahu ran through the city shouting: "Whoever is zealous for the Torah and is steadfast in the Covenant let him follow me!" (I Maccabees 2.27).

Mattisyahu, his sons and many who sought to live according to righteousness fled to the mountains and settled in the Judean Desert (I Maccabees 2.28-30). Stay tuned, because tomorrow we will go into the battle that the Maccabees had to fight to even get to the place of re-dedicating God's Altar in Jerusalem. It is a prophetic foreshadow of our own arduous battle to re-dedicate our hearts fully to the One True God.

Discussion Questions:

1. Why is it important to understand the Abomination of Desolation?

2. Why do you think God had Daniel prophesy about the first named Antichrist – Antiochus Epiphanes IV – 300 years before he came on the scene? Why did Jesus refer to Daniel's prophecy and point to the greater abomination in the end of days?

*****

DAY 3 – Journey to Become His Bride: History of Hanukkah – Part II

"You also, as living stones, build up yourselves and become spiritual temples and holy priests to offer up spiritual sacrifices acceptable to God by Jesus Christ" (1 Peter 2.5 Aramaic).

The difficult battle to re-dedicate one's heart fully to God in this Kingdom Day is foreshadowed by the five battles that the Maccabees fought prior to making it to Jerusalem.

Did you know that historically the first Hanukkah highlights Judah the Maccabee and his band of faithful men? Had this small ragtag remnant not taken their courageous stand against the Antichrist of their day and had they not overcome overwhelming odds to save their culture and religion from utter annihilation, both Judaism and Christianity most likely would not exist today.

Let's begin where we left off yesterday. A righteous son of a High Priest refused to desecrate "The Name" by sacrificing a pig on God's Altar. The zeal of the Lord consumed Mattisyahu when one of his countrymen, who was supposed to be set apart, tried to make a pagan sacrifice in his stead. Not only did Mattisyahu slat the Jew upon the makeshift pagan altar, but he slew the pagan king's emissary as well. After tearing down the pagan altar set up in his little town of Modin, Mattisyahu ran through the streets shouting "Whoever is zealous for the Torah and is steadfast in the Covenant let him follow me!" (I Maccabees 2.27).

Mattisyahu, his sons and many who sought to live according to righteousness fled to the mountains and settled in the Judean Desert (I Maccabees 2.28-30). They left all their worldly possession. Antiochus' forces could not disregard this challenge to their authority. Six thousand combat-ready Jews gathered under Mattisyahu's banner. They began to strike back be destroying idolatrous altars in nocturnal raids (1 Maccabees 2.45).

Mattisyahu dies within a year in 166 B.C. He did not see the results of what had been set in motion; but before the patriarch died, he gathered his five sons: Shimon (Simon), Yehudah (Judah), Elazar (Eleazar), Yochanan (John) and Yonasan (Jonathan). He urges them to stand steadfast and continue the good fight against the Syrian Greeks (I Maccabees 2.49-69). Mattisyahu's last words established Shimon as *"a wise man; listen to him always"* and Judah *"a warrior from his youth shall be the leader of your army and direct the war against the nations" (I Maccabees 3.65-66).*

The official appointed to administer Judea – Philip – did not take the Mattisyahu revolt seriously. He felt they could be contained by the troops stationed in the vicinity of Judea. Philip first called up Apollonius, the military commander of Samaria. Before Apollonius and the Cutheans could attack, Judah was forewarned and struck first killing Apollonius with much of his army (I Maccabees

3.10-12).

Second, Seron the commander of the army in Syria heard about the Maccabee revolt, and he decided to gain a reputation by crushing Judah (I Maccabees 3.13-14). Seron gathered a large and well-equipped army and marched to Judea. As Seron approached Beth Choron, Judah and his men saw Seron's vats army. Judah's men had been fasting and were frightened, but Judah remembering his father's final words reassured the men: *"It is easy for the many to be handed over to the few, for there is no difference in God's eyes between saving through a large force or through a tiny force. Triumph in battle does not depend on the size of an army – for strength comes from heaven. Our enemy opposes us full of violence and lawlessness, to destroy us, our wives and our children, and to plunder us. But we are fighting for our lives and our Torah. God will crush them before us and you must not fear them!" (I Maccabees 3.18-22).* When Judah finished speaking, he wasted no time by suddenly rushing Seron's army crushing them (I Maccabees 3.23). The enemy's plan became their portion.

Upon hearing about his troops defeat by a bunch of circumcised nincompoops, Antiochus flew into another rage. He commanded that his entire army gather together. He opened his treasure chests and paid his soldiers a full year's wages. Antiochus then realized that his coffers had been depleted through his military campaigns and his lavish spending for banquets, grandiose buildings and gladiator games. So King Antiochus was advised to go to Persia to collect tribute owed him while Lysias was entrusted with the care of the young heir to the throne (Antiochus V Eupator).

Antiochus IV equipped half the army with war elephants (the ancient equivalent of tanks) and assigned them to Lysias' command with orders to march on Judea and crush the Jewish nation. Lysias promptly appointed three of Syria's ablest generals: Ptolemy son of Dorimenes, Nikanor and Gorgias. He put them in charge of 40,000 foot soldiers and 7,000 cavalries. They marched into Judea as far as Emmaus (I Maccabees 3.27-40). Emmaus is the town where Yeshua would later reveal himself to His disciples after His resurrection. Once they recognized Him in the breaking of bread, Yeshua disappeared.

So confident were the Syrian Greeks of their victory that Nikanor had summoned slave dealers from the coastal cities and promised them Jewish slaves at an unprecedently low price. Instead of Judah losing heart, the faithful band of Maccabean brothers went to Mitzpah to fast and pray. Mitzpah was a city that had been a place of prayer for God's salvation in the days of Samuel.

As they all fasted and prayed, *"they unrolled the scroll of the law, to learn about the things for which Gentiles consulted the images of their idols. They brought with them the priestly vestments (kings and priests of the Order of Melchizedek take note), the first fruits, and the tithes; and brought forward the Nazarites who had completed the time of their vows. And they cried aloud to Heaven: 'What shall we do with these men, and where shall we take them'* For *Your sanctuary has been trampled on and profaned, and Your priests are in mourning and humiliation. Now the Gentiles are gathered together against us to destroy us. How shall we be able to resist them unless You help us?' Then they blew the trumpets and cried loudly" (I Maccabees 3.48-54).*

Judah appointed officers over thousands, over hundred, over fifties and over tens. They camped south of Emmaus, as Judah exhorted the troops: *"Arm yourselves and be brave; in the morning, be ready to fight these Gentiles who have assembled against us to destroy us and our sanctuary. Whatever heaven wills, He will do" (I Maccabees 3.57-59).*

At daybreak, Judah and 3,000 ill-equipped men see the vast expanse of expert soldiers. Judah exhorts his ragtag remnant again: *"Do not be afraid of their numbers or dread their attack. Remember how our fathers were saved in the Red Sea, when Pharaoh pursued them with an army" (I Maccabees 4.8-9).* The foreigners come out for battle when they look up and see the Maccabees marching toward them. When the men of Judah blow the trumpet, as one, the Syrians' orderly phalanxes dissolve and the Jews decimate the rear guard. They set the Syrian camp on fire, and keep pursuing the enemy a long way. Judah cautions his men that a large part of the enemy is still in the mountains, but Gorgias and his troops flee the battlefield once they see fire rising from their main camp.

After Lysias licks his wounds for a year (165 B.C.), he sends a stronger force of 60,000 infantry and 5,000 cavalry. Judah and his band of faith-filled men meet them at Beth Tzur with 10,000 loyal Jews. Again, Judah appeals to heaven when he sees their vastly greater force: *"Blessed are You, O, Savior of Israel, who halted the charge of the Philistine champion, Goliath, through Your servant David and who delivered a Philistine camp into the hands of Jonathan ben Saul and his armor bearer. Do the same to this camp – let them be ashamed of their army and their cavalry. Make them cowardly, melt their boldness, make them tremble at their imminent destruction. Strike them down with the sword of those who love You and let all who know Your Name sing praises to You" (I Maccabees 4.30-33).* Hand-to-hand combat ensues and approximately 5,000 of Lysias' men are killed. Seeing the determination of the Jews where they would rather die than surrender, Lysias withdraws his troops back to Antioch in Syria. When Judah sees that the Syrian Greeks will not mount another offensive in the foreseeable future, he tells his brothers: *"Let us go up to purify the sanctuary and re-dedicate it" (I Maccabees 4.36).*

It's time to go up!!! It's time to go up to the Jerusalem above to present oneself as a pure and living sacrifice. If the powers-that-be-of-this-world have tried to hide the importance of the re-dedication of God's Altar, don't you think that we should pay particular attention to it?

It is no coincidence that God faith-filled sons have to battle the world's superpower (the Antichrist) to save the culture of the Kingdom of God; and it's a small remnant doing the work. The Antichrist sets up his own high priest in God's Temple while the job of the Order of Melchizedek is to set up Yeshua Ha Machiach (Jesus

Christ) as the sole High Priest in our Temple. Don't you know that you are the Temple of God (1 Corinthians 3.17)?

The Order of Melchizedek is made up of sons of righteousness who build His Temple and "offer up spiritual sacrifices acceptable to God by Jesus Christ" (1 Peter 2.5). The wife of the Lamb is His Dwelling Place (Revelation 21.3). She is one with the All-Consuming Fire being a continual fiery sacrifice – a Blazing Fire Bride.

May we press through these arduous battles to re-dedicate the altars of our hearts as well as our bodies. May re-dedicate them to the One who deserves all the glory!

Discussion Questions:

1. How do you and I set up our own high priest in God's Temple - us?

2. Why do you need to present yourself as a living sacrifice?

*****

DAY 4 – Priests Cleansing Our Temples

"But you are a chosen people, ministers to the kingdom, a holy people. A congregation redeemed to proclaim the glories of Him who has called you out of darkness to His marvelous light" (1 Peter 2.9 Aramaic).

Hanukkah celebrates the purification of God's Temple, which was the preeminent house of worship in Jerusalem. The Bible also tells us that believers are the Temple of the Holy Spirit. *"Or do you not know that your body is the temple of the Holy Spirit, who lives in you and was given to you by God? You do not belong to yourself, for God bought you with a high price. So you must honor God with your body" (1 Corinthians 6.19-20 NLT).* The flame of the Holy Spirit burns inside and outside of us, so we may be the light of the world.

It as the priests that cleansed the Temple the first Hanukkah. When we review the below characteristics of the Levitical Priesthood, we can see some original requirements of the Lord that are still necessary for hos royal priesthood today. These priestly characteristics will show us areas in our own lives that can use some improvement or cleansing. Let us look at the Levites to gain some understanding about the priesthood that believers belong to, and the behavior expected for God's holy nation. The Tribe of Levi was chosen by God to be set apart for intimate relationship with God:

[1] The Levites were set apart, because they were willing to pay the price to go against the flow. The radically obeyed the Lord (Exodus 32). They took a painful stand of righteousness that was a sword against their brothers.

[2] The Levites were God centered (Numbers 3). The Levites camped around the Presence of God, not around a person, doctrine, group, etc.

[3] They gave up the right to a "normal" life. The Lord Himself became their inheritance.

[4] They had cities of refuge, where broken0hearted, hurting people had a safe place to come.

[5] The Levites' first ministry was, and is, to the Lord (Ezekiel 44.10-16).

[6] They led continual worship in the Tabernacle/Temple. There was a special song for each day as well as specific songs for festivals, sacrifices and offerings. Jewish tradition say that when the Lord "spoke" the world into existence, He actually sung it.

[7] The Levites brought the Presence of God back to Jerusalem and all cities (1 Chronicles 15). God's people radically obey Him, and their lives are centered on Him.

Discussion Questions:

1. In what way(s) can you cleanse your temple?

2. What priestly characteristic speaks to you the most?

*****

DAY 5 – Winter One-der-land Portal Resonating with Great Grace

"For who are you, O great mountain of human obstacles? Before Zerubbabel who with Joshua had led the return of the exiles from Babylon and was undertaking the rebuilding of the temple, before him you shall become a mere molehill! And he shall bring forth the finishing gable stone of the new temple with loud shouting of the people, crying, Grace, grace to it!" (Zechariah 4.7 Amplified).

The ideal and quintessential verse for Hanukkah is Zechariah 4.6. It communicates that above the might and power exerted to win the battle to purify one's heart and body is the reality that this work needs to be done by the Spirit of the Living God: *"Not by might, nor by power, but by My Spirit, says the Lord of hosts" (Zechariah 4.6).*

Hanukkah is an Ancient Golden Gate of Thanksgiving and Awe, which is prepared for His special season of lights, miracles and dedicating our temple to walk as Yeshua did.

Every year this Hanukkah portal opens to a greater grace to become one with the King of Kings and the Lord of Lords. His Winter One-der-land portal not only resonates with the awesome, reverential fear of the Lord, but with great grace.

His great miracle-working grace enables the wings of His heart to wrap around your eyes, so that you can realize how He truly sees any situation or person, including yourself. The Lord told me that the wings of His heart wrapping around your eyes opens a window of His Spirit to literally behold how His heart moves. Talk about not by might or power, but by His Spirit!

Grace has a purpose, and that purpose is obedience: *"the gospel concerning His Son, who was descended from David according to the to the flesh designated Son of God in power according to the Spirit of holiness by His resurrection from the dead, Jesus Christ our Lord, through whom we have* RECEIVED GRACE *and apostleship* TO BRING ABOUT THE OBEDIENCE *of faith for the sake of His Name among the nations" (Romans 1.3-5 RSV).*

Great grace is even more so. Great grace is pictured in Romans 6 where we see obedience leading to righteousness and righteousness leading to holiness: *"16 Know ye not, that to whom ye yield yourselves servants to obey, his servants ye are to whom you obey; whether of sin unto death, or of obedience unto righteousness?[19] I speak after the manner of men because of the infirmity of your flesh: for as have yielded your members servants to uncleanness and to iniquity unto iniquity; even so yield your members servants of righteousness unto holiness" (Romans 6.16,19 KJV).*

"Being holy, as He is holy" (1 Peter 1.16) is not a suggestion, but a command. Once Moses and company built the Tabernacle in the Wilderness (the Book of Exodus), they were instructed about the protocols of Temple Life in which holiness is key (Book of Leviticus).

The minimal requirements for holiness for the sons of the Living God were given to the church three times in the Book of Acts by the Jerusalem Counsel. The Apostolic Decree, listed in Acts 15.20, Acts 15.29, and Acts 21.25, contain the four essential abstinence requirements for all believers in the Lord Jesus Christ. These essential commandments for all believers prohibit thing that have had, or currently have, connections to pagan customs and traditions. They are abstinence requirements to live a holy life, just as abstinence before marriage preserves the sanctity of holy matrimony. Amazing as it may seem (since the church has greatly lost track of these essential commandments for all believers), these abstinence requirements for the Bride of Christ preserve the sanctity of holy matrimony to our Bridegroom. For more information, please refer to http://wp.me/p158HG-AT.

The Bride of Christ epitomizes the Dwelling Place of God: *"[2]And I John saw the holy city, New Jerusalem, coming down from God out of heaven, prepared as a bride adorned for husband. 3And I heard a great voice out of heaven saying, Behold the Tabernacle of God is with men, and He will dwell with them, and they shall be His people, and God Himself shall be with them, and be their God" (Revelation 21.2-3 KJV).* Listen to the great grace language that Zechariah speaks of rebuilding of God's Temple:

> *"[6] Then he said to me, This addition of the bowl to the candlestick, causing it to yield a ceaseless supply of oil from the olive trees is the word of the Lord to Zerubabbel saying, NOT BY MIGHT, NOR BY POWER, BUT BY MY SPIRIT of whom the oil is a symbol, says the Lord of hosts. [7] FOR WHO ARE YOU, O GREAT MOUNTAIN OF HUMAN OBSTACLES? Before Zerubbabel who with Joshua had led the return of the exiles from Babylon and was undertaking the rebuilding of the temple, before him you shall become a mere molehill! And HE SHALL BRING FOR THE FINISHING GABLE STONE OF THE NEW TEMPLE with loud shouting of the people, CRYING, GRACE, GRACE TO IT!"*
> *(Zechariah 4.6-7 Amplified).*

May you and yours receive and operate in His great miracle-working grace!

Discussion Questions:

1. Why would you tap into His portal of great grace?

2. Where do you need great grace to in re-dedicating your altar (heart) and your (temple)?

*****

DAY 6 – Yeshua Celebrated Hanukkah, Not Christmas

"And when Aaron saw the molten calf, he built an altar before it; and Aaron made proclamation, and said, Tomorrow shall be a feast to the Lord" *(Exodus 32.5 Aramaic).*

I have heard people repeatedly say that Hukkah has nothing to do with Christmas, but that is simply not the case. Hanukkah is all about overthrowing a polluted sacrificial system instituted in God's Temple that centers around sun god worship, which is essentially Christmas. Throughout antiquity all pagan sun gods' birthdays have been celebrated on the ancient winter solstice – December 25th. This is the exact day that the Antichrist prophesied by Daniel erected a pagan sun god statue on God's Altar defiling it. Today, it is the same day that most Christians offer up the same pagan sun god deity in their hearts without knowing its origins. Your heart is God's Altar where the ultimate battle for purity is being fought.

Yeshua did not celebrate His birth – Christmas. He celebrated Hanukkah, which commemorates the overthrow of Christmas – pagan sun god worship. Today most Christians are actually doing what the first Antichrist did and calling it true worship.

We can claim that we truly worship Yeshua (Jesus) through Christmas, but like the Golden Calf, He sees to the roots of our self-proclaimed feast said to be dedicated to Jehovah (Exodus 32.5). The first recorded evidence of a supposed "Christian: Christmas is found in 336 A.D. during the time of the world-dominating corrupt Constantine.

God's shekinah dwelling presence literally requires holiness. We have talked extensively about the most immediate predecessor of today's Christmas Day celebration was originally Mithra's Winter Festival celebrated on the ancient winter solstice December 25th. This pagan-Christian mixture is not only unholy, but it tethers God's unlimited people to the limited illusion of three-dimensional space and the fourth dimension of time. When you accept Jesus Christ as your Lord and Savior, eternity, in the form of Jesus and the Holy Spirit, was placed in your heart, which means you have been released into a non-local, eternal reality where you can literally be any place in the multiverse at any time. Much more is at stake than some tinsel, gifts and manger scene on your mantle.

Christians can say that your Christmas worship is not pagan sun god worship (i.e., idolatry) and believe it to the hilt; but understand that He will have the last say. This is not a salvation issue. It is about eternal rewards and being part of Christ's Bride. God will only attach Himself to things like Him: *"And what agreement has the Temple of God with idols? For you are the Temple of the Living God. As God has said: 'I will dwell in them and walk among them. I will be their God, and they shall be My people'" (2 Corinthians 6.16 NKJV).*

Discussion Questions:

1. Have you ever thought about the Hanukkah celebrating the overthrow of Christmas and the re-dedication of God's Altar and Temple?

2. If you are a follower of Jesus and He celebrated Hanukkah, what impact does this have upon you and your family?

*****

DAY 7 – Destroy the Wall of Self-Protection

"But it is He who knows my way and mu existence,
and has tried me like gold, and I came forth pure" (Job 23.10 Aramaic).

The biggest end-time battle is fought on the soil of SELF. It's a war between the Holy Three in One (Father, Son and Holy Spirit) and the Unholy Threesome in me – me, myself and I. I say this for many reasons, but here I'd like to point out that "The Satanic Bible" proclaims: "On this new age, the only moral commandment will be, 'Do what thou wilt shall be the whole of the law.'" The Satanic Kingdom can literally be equated to the Kingdom of Self. What many people don't realize is the Babylon is focused on "self" as well: *"The Babylonians, that ruthless and impetuous people, who sweep across the earth… They are a law to themselves… whose strength is their god" (Habakkuk 1.6,7,11).*

Keep in mind that the Hebrew Word Picture (Pictograph) for the word "pride" tells us that pride is to lift up yourself in your own strength, while the Hebrew Word Picture for "humility" shows us that humility comes when you destroy your wall of self-protection. Please note that "self" is the key ingredient that determines whether one is full of pride or humility.

As Yeshua and I tore down my wall of self-protection through me endeavoring to stay humble and teachable, He taught me more and more of His glorious irresistible love. I remember crossing the street one day, when it hit me. I told Him with a forlorn tone, "I don't even know how to love." His response: "What a great place to start. Finally, we can begin."

We worked and worked and worked together in a labor of love. Then one day Yeshua came to me and told me that I had done a good job working to destroy my wall of self-protection by trying to stay open and running to Him for shelter in life's storm; then He placed a thorn in my heart and told me that this is what I needed for the wall of self-protection in me to be completely destroyed.

For ten years, I forgot about the thorn that my Love had placed in my heart. I'd like to sun up the experience in a few lines, but He desires a greater amount of detail. First, let me preface that we can and should work at destroying our walls of self-protection (as unto the Lord), but our final deliverance comes through a crucifixion process.

The Lord led me to be in silent servant mode for several years in a congregation that my family attended for 15 years. Prior to being released to go to a Sunday Night Prophetic Prayer Gathering, Yeshua had told me that when I step out in my apostolic-prophetic-teaching anointing again that I was going to get hit. So, needless to say, I was on high alert. There was an open mic that night, but knowing that something was probably coming I okayed what I was getting from the Lord with the lead pastor before I stepped out. He assured me that it was an open mic led by the Spirit, so I led a prayer for a friend who had just lost his father. I thought: "Okay. That wasn't so bad." Then the lead pastor got up and started sharing what God gave him. I got a sinking feeling, because what the Lord gave me in the car ride over there perfectly dovetailed with what he was sharing. I recognized the Holy Spirit's scarlet cord. So… I sauntered over to a good mature friend, and told her my dilemma. She assured me that if God gave it to me, then just obey. So… I swallowed hard. Pulled up my breeched to rein in any fear and released da love.

My piece was very simple and small. I told all present that night that we can all experience God. We can see, hear, and perceive what the Spirit of the Lord is saying, according to the gifts deposited in each one of us. All we need to do is get in right alignment. Bu our will, we can choose to have our bodies submit to our souls, our souls submit to our spirits, and our spirits submit to the Holy Spirit. I was also led to say that our spirit intersects with our soul at our will. That's why "not my will, but Thine be done" is such a powerful kingdom concept. Let's so this, so They Kingdom come! They will be done!

I finished my little part, and was relieved that I was still in one piece. I thought maybe I had heard the Lord wrong, until I went to the back of the room. After I hugged a girlfriend and told her how much Jesus loved her, I stepped back to enter into a prayerful, worship-filled stance when I noticed that there was a shadow to the left of me. So, I stepped to my right to avoid it. As I did, I felt my left arm being grabbed real hard; and then, I was shook around like a rag doll. After the other pastor shook and shook me, he raged at me and told me that he didn't want me ministering to anyone. I was so clam inside, as I stared in amazement as a Jezebel Spirit that was manifesting right in front of my eyes. I remember being more concerned with the spiritual than the natural at the time. As I told him. "I don't know what you're talking about. I've okayed what I am doing with the lead pastor," he stormed away, as I sunk into the back wall, stunned to say the least. When both pastors came to me, I was checking in with the Lord trying to understand what was going on. When the lead pastor pointed at me and said, "I will have no division in my church. You two work it out." I thought something like: "Great. I'm being thrown into the lion's den."

I went with the abusive pastor into the foyer. The first thing he said was "I am the door. You must come through me." I just stared that man down. Incensed that He would defame My Love's Word like that and use it as an excuse to abuse someone, especially since there were so many young people in the church. When I didn't budge and didn't appear to be afraid, the pastor came to himself for a moment and said, "I mean Jesus is the door." Then he flipped back to being controlled by Jezzy and proclaimed, "But you must come through me.

Yeshua had previously taught me that when someone inserts themselves into your life for evil or destruction, you have the right in the Spirit to insert yourself in their life to bring about their redemption. It's a glorious way to overcome evil with good. That is what I was led to do that entire night at church.

Long story, short. I tossed and turned all night. Yeshua kept on telling me to run into Him. It took all my will to do so, because I literally wanted to run inside myself and hide. About 3:00 the next afternoon, I finally could not take it any longer and I cried out to the Lord for help from the depths of my being. Immediately, as searing bright laser light descended from heaven and burned a layer off me. I just knew that my final layer of self-protection was gone; then I remembered the thorn that Yeshua had placed in my heart.

In hindsight, I knew that the thorn eventually attracted a crucifixion experience; but I also felt the reverential fear of the Lord with the message of "woe" to the man through whom it would come. This experience could have delivered him too, but I discovered in this experience that by the time an authority figure abuses another person publicly, they are pretty far gone. Repentance and redemption were available and I was praying my heart out, but they were too busy trying to keep me in line and keep their own kingdom intact to look at their own heart and actions. Please note: Our message to others means nothing if we don't love others first and foremost.

There was a time in my life when I needed self-protection in hurtful and abusive situations. It's a way God has designed for all of us to survive when we don't know what else to do. But now I choose LOVE. I choose humility. I choose to be teachable. I choose my Rock, my Fortress, and my Deliverer, my God in whom I can trust. *"When I was a child, I spoke as a child, I understood as a child, I thought as a child; but when I became a man, I put away childish things: (1 Corinthians 13.11 NKJV).*

All Kingdom Hearts are growing into the image of His Mature Body, which will grow beyond the darkness of the Kingdom of Self. If one looks in the dictionary, there are over 100 words with the word "self" in front of them. Each one can be thought of as steps up a Babylonian ziggurat (pyramid) to exult self. Self-protection is just one of these steps, but… oh… what a stumbling stone.

The first verse that I memorized at Big Sky Bible Camp after I was saved at 7 years old was John 3.16. The second verse was *Job 23.10: "But He know that way that I take; when He has tested me, I shall come forth as gold."* Keep on pressing onward and upward to the mark of the high calling in Christ Jesus. Dear Heart, you shall come forth as gold!!!

Discussion Questions:

1. How is destroying the wall of self-protection related to re-dedicating your heart and cleansing your temple?

2. Why does God use crucifying experiences to set us free?

*****

DAY 8 – The Bride is Clothed as She Walks

"[1] LORD, who may abide in Your Tabernacle? Who may dwell in Your holy hill? [2] He who walks uprightly, and works righteousness, and speaks the truth in his heart" (Psalm 15:1-2 NKJV).

The very first time that I was caught up in a corporate ascension, as the Bride of Christ, I saw an attic door open up early and Yeshua peeked down. He asked if I'd like to come up early. I hesitated; then I realized it was Him. Yeshua reached down, as I reached up. When we touched, I was immediately with Him in the Spirit.

Yeshua said, "Let's wait here for the rest of them." I looked around. We were on purple clouds and the stars above were bright. Yeshua sat cross-legged and invited me to do the same. Shortly, He exclaimed, "Come on!" as He took my hand and pulled me to my feet. We started to walk side-by-side; then He stepped in front as I followed. We walked and walked and walked and walked and walked and walked. We walked as Nancy Coen (the leader of the group) declared, "The window is open!"

I looked up, because a glaring brightness became visible in another layer of clouds above us. Yeshua led. I followed. As I climbed through the radiant opening, we were encompassed with light. Nothing else was visible. I remember knowing at the time that He and I had become one – the same essence.

As soon as I was aware of oneness, I saw myself plainly dressed in a white dressing room looking into a mirror. The door opened and in stepped Jesus. He presented me with a simple gold necklace. Yeshua said, "For purity," as He raised the necklace up and asked me to turn around. I turned around and raised my hair. Yeshua hooked the gold necklace and promptly exited the dressing room.

When I saw a simple white undergarment above my head, I raised my arms to receive it. Then I waited for a while longer. Something inside of me prompted me to get up and open the dressing room door. I started to walk clothed only in my white camisole and gold necklace. As I walked, different pieces of my wedding dress flung unto me; my upper left sleeve, lower right sleeve, etc. My wedding dress was simple, but elegant. It was white and sparkled. Just as I reached out to grab the handle to this huge wooden door, the last piece, completing my ensemble, flung unto me. I was fully, properly, and gloriously clothed.

I opened the door and immediately saw myself at the left side of Yeshua, just as my wedding ring sits on my left hand. Yeshua and I were sitting at the banqueting table. I knew that there must have been a most sumptuous feast, but I truly didn't care, for I only had eyes for Him. I was literally "lost" in His eyes. I had a vague recollection that there must be people in attendance, but I just could not take my eyes off of Him. Everything paled in comparison.

After a little while, Yeshua told me to stand. I did. Then He told me to take a bow. I replied, "You are the One that is supposed to bow. You do it all." My Love repeated kindly, yet unwaveringly, "Bow, My dear. I want to honor My Bride." I could not deny His easy request. As I simply and humbly bowed, the whole of heaven applauded. I was so overwhelmed. I remember that I looked at Him and He was all smiles. He was so magnificent and truly deserved all the glory and honor and praise. Yet, here He was sharing it all."

- *"[1] LORD, who may abide in Your Tabernacle? Who may dwell in Your holy hill? [2] He who walks uprightly, and works righteousness, and speaks the truth in his heart" (Psalm 15.1-2 NKJV).*

- *"[7] Let us be glad and rejoice and give Him glory, for the marriage of the Lamb has come, and His wife has made herself ready. [8] And to her it was granted to be arrayed in fine linen, clean and bright, for the fine linen is the righteous acts of the saints" (Revelation 18.7-8 NKJV).*

- *"[5] But whoever keeps His word, truly the love of God is perfected in him. By this we know that we are in Him. [6] He who says he abides in Him ought himself also to walk just as He walked" (1 John 2.5-6 NKJV).*

- *"[22] Now it was the Feast of Dedication in Jerusalem, and it was winter. [23] And Jesus walked in the Temple, in Solomon's Porch" (John 10.22-23 NKJV).*

Discussion Questions:

1. Why is the Bride clothed as she walks?
2. Who do you think is at the marriage of the Lamb?

*****

8 – MYSTERY OF INIQUITY VS. MYSTERY OF LOVE

DAY 1 – Mysteries of His Love

"And you shall love the LORD your God with all your heart and with all your soul and all your might" (Deuteronomy 6.5 Aramaic).

The invitation is going out to get lost in the mystery of His love. For indeed, love is an endless mystery where we shall lose it all in order to find ourselves in Him. *"Many waters cannot quench love, neither can the rivers carry it away; and yet, if a man would give all the substance of his house for love, people would mock him" (Song of Solomon 8.7 Aramaic).*

The glorious path through His Winter One-der-land is paved with mystery. A treasure trove of the mystery of His will for the purpose of gathering all things together in one in Christ: *"[7] In Him we have salvation, and in His blood, forgiveness of sins, according to the richness of His grace, [8] That that grace which has abounded to us, in all wisdom and spiritual understanding,* [9] *And made known to us the mystery of His will that He ordained from the very beginning, to work through it;* [10] *As a dispensation of the fullness of times, that all things might be made new in heaven and on earth through Christ" (Ephesians 1.7-10 Aramaic).*

Not only does Scripture speak of the mysteries of God's Kingdom, but its antithesis Mystery, Babylon the Great and its accompanying mystery of iniquity. The choice is ours to make. Choose this day who you will serve – the Mysteries of God, the Metatron Messiah Yeshua and His Kingdom – OR – Mystery Babylon. In spite of the institutional church's ardent efforts to bury the truth about its assimilation of Babylonian tradition, reference after reference can be sited of Christmas' connection to Mystery Babylon.

The first time that God's people came out of Babylon was at the Tower of Babel where they had been trying to make a name for themselves (Genesis 11.4). The Bible says that the people of Babel exerted a tremendous amount of energy building a tower of bricks – lest they be scattered. What they feared actually happened. The year of the dispersion of the seventy nations from the Tower of Babel has been recorded in Hebrew History to be 340 years after the flood. Noah, Shem, Ham, and Japheth were still alive; and Abraham was 48 years old. *"But as the days of Noah were, so also will the coming of the Son of Man be" (Matthew 24.37 NKJV).*

The next time the set apart people of God Most High come out of Babylon, they will also have one heart and one mind; but this time, unlike the first time, God's Holy Priesthood of believers will truly be set on loving the Lord our God with all their heart, souls and strength (Deuteronomy 6.5). This Bridal Company will be one with a common purpose to make God's name great – totally surrendering all to Him and His Kingdom ways. Coming out of Babylon in this Kingdom Day will result in the One New Man in the Messiah coming into its fullness, as Metatron Messiah (Ephesians 2.15; Ephesians 3.14). For more information on Metatron, please refer to the *MEL GEL Study Guide* => https://www.amazon.com/dp/0578188538/. To come into the fullness of the One New Man in Christ, we must forsake all, but the Lord; then He will ONEdrously make heaven and earth His Sons of Righteousness' oyster.

The invitation has gone out for the mystery of His love: *"Blessed are those invited to the wedding feast of the Lamb" (Revelation 19.9 NLT)*. Obedience to God's truth and righteousness will bring each of us into the beauty of holiness. Won't you lose it all that you may find yourself in Him?

Discussion Questions:

1. What mystery has been revealed to you recently?

2. What could be better than losing oneself in the mystery of His love?

*****

DAY 2 – Coals of Fire from Blazing New Wine

"Set me as a seal upon thine heart, as a seal upon thine arm: for love is strong as death; jealousy is cruel as the grave: the coals thereof are coals of fire, which hath a most vehement flame" (Song of Solomon 8.6 KJV).

Who would have guessed that one short and sweet reference to Yeshua's (Jesus) celebration of Hanukkah in John 10.22-23 is a major key to so many kingdom mysteries? In fact, there's a major chuck of Scripture where Yeshua is at the Feasts of Dedication (John 8.12-John 10.39). Most ancient texts put the passage about the woman caught in the act of adultery during the Feast of Tabernacles (John 8.1-11). We also have two fairly accurate historical books to go by. These books are called *First Maccabees* and *Second Maccabees* in *The Apocrypha.* The events surrounding the first Hanukkah as well as Yeshua's celebration of it foreshadow the pouring out of a blazing new wine in our day.

So, let the coals of fire from the blazing new wine of Hanukkah go forth from YHVH and be scattered upon your earth and mine. Let His judgments be executed, so we will know "I AM." Don't forget that the Ancient Hebrew Word Picture for the word "judge" communicates that the Judge is the Door of Life – Yeshua. He only judges things that hinder love, life and light:

- *"[2] O LORD, I have heard Thy speech, and was afraid: O LORD, revive thy work in the midst of the years make known; in wrath remember mercy… [4] And His brightness was as the light; He had horns coming out of His hand; and there was the hiding of His power. [5] Before Him went the pestilence, and burning coals went forth at His feet. [6] He stood, and measured the earth: He beheld, and drove asunder the nations; and everlasting mountains were scattered, the perpetual hills did bow: His ways are everlasting" (Habakkuk 3.2, 4-6 KJV).*

- *"[8] Then the earth shook and trembled; the foundations of heaven moved and shook, because He was wroth. [9] There went up a smoke out of His nostrils, and fire out of His mouth devoured: coals were kindled by it. [10] He bowed the heavens also, and came down; and darkness was under His feet. [11] And He rode upon a cherub and did fly: and he was seen upon the wings of the wind" (2 Samuel 22.8-11 KJV).*

The cherub or cherubim that God is riding upon in this Kingdom Day are made up of wings of God's End-Time Melchizedek Army who fly by the Spirit of the Living God together. These kings and priests of the Most High

God are a New Living Creature. They are returning to their primordial state where Adam and Eve lived and moved and had their being before the Fall, except better. They will have been redeemed. In their fullness, they will be a Full Age or Mature One New Man in the Messiah (i.e., Metatron). The multimembered fully mature Body of Christ will be complete morally, complete emotionally, complete mentally, complete in labor and complete in growth. Please refer to the "Formation of the New Living Creature" video for more information about "cherub: or "cherubim" => https://www.youtube.com/watch?v=1BElDZaaFqpo.

Know that His coals of fire are His coals of love: "*Set me as a seal upon thine heart, as a seal upon thine arm: for love is strong as death; jealousy is cruel as the grave: the coals thereof are coals of fire, which hath a most vehement flame" (Song of Solomon 8.6 KJV).* Also, know that the coals of fire from the blazing new wine of Hanukkah has been created by Him: *"Behold, I have created the smith that blows the coals of fire…" (Isaiah 54.16)*, and within the fire of discipline are the embers of restoration. There was a fire of coals at both Peter's denial and his restoration (John 18.17-18; John 21.9). Please note that His judgments are disciplines until His final judgment.

Hear He! Hear He! Hear He! Yeshua is even now gathering set apart hearts that have been washed by His blood. He is carrying willing hearts to His Great Feasts of Love, which are His Biblical Feasts. Here's the catch. It's for willing hearts only. Will you forsake all, but Him?

During Hanukkah, Yeshua risked life and limb to go up to Jerusalem to celebrate this particular feast with believers. Why? Why did Yeshua choose Hanukkah as the time to break every man-made tradition (i.e., man-made law) that could apply when He healed a man born blind" Why did He choose Hanukkah to fulfill perhaps the truest sign that He was the Messiah?

Discussion Questions:

1. Why is His coals of fire are His coals of love?

2. How does discipline mature God's sons?

*****

DAY 3 – Hanukkah Marker to Calculate Fulfillment of the Antichrist

"[9] The coming of the lawless one is according to the working of Satan, with all power, signs, and lying wonders, [10] and with all unrighteous deception among those who perish, because they did not receive the love of the truth, that they might be saved. [11] And for this reason God will send them strong delusion, [12] that they should believe the lie" (2 Thessalonians 2.9-12 NJKV).

Did you know that the story of Hanukkah begins in the Book of Daniel 300 years before the event took place" In fact, we did not have the markers on the calendar to be able to calculate the fulfillment of the Antichrist being revealed until both Purim and Hanukkah were put in place?

Yeshua Himself attaches a prophetic significance to the Feast of Dedication (Hanukkah) by telling us that the first Abomination of Desolation (Antichrist) is a prophetic foreshadow of an even greater abomination that confronts the believer in the last days? Come! Let's seek to understand what the Pattern Son has to say about the Antichrist and His Bride.

Matthew chapters 23-24 happen on an afternoon when Yeshua steps out of the Temple in Jerusalem giving the Pharisees almost no recourse but to kill Him. The Bible tells us that thousands of people were following Yeshua before He went up to Jerusalem. When Yeshua was on the Temple Mount that day, thousands of His disciples were with Him as well as hundred-of-thousands people. This is when Yeshua lays the Pharisees bare. He tells His disciples do not follow the Pharisees, and calls them all sorts of names. Refer to Matthew 23.1-2, 13, 14, 15, 16-17, 21, 23-33.

By the time that Yeshua storms out of the Temple with His disciples, He completely exposed the religious leader of His day calling them sons of heel and a brood of vipers. Yeshua leaves telling the Scribes and Pharisees that they are not going to see Him again until they break their own rule against saying the Name: *"for I say to you, you shall see Me no more till you say, 'Blessed is He who comes in the Name of the LORD!" (Matthew 23.29 NKJV).*

As Yeshua and His disciples are on their way out, His nervous disciples point out the beautiful work being done on Herod's Temple. Then Yeshua remarks: *"Assuredly, I say to you, not one stone shall be left here upon another, that shall not be thrown down" (Matthew 24.2 NKJV)*. After Yeshua said that, no one opened their mouths as they walked down the Temple Mount, down the Kidron Valley, across the brook until they arrive on the Mount of Olives. Once they all sat down, the disciples asked Him: *"Tell us, when will these things be? And what will be the sign of Your coming, and of the end of the age?" (Matthew 24.3 NKJV)*. The first thing Yeshua counsels them is: *"Take heed that no one deceives you" (Matthew 24.4 NKJV)*. Everything in Matthew 24 is in regard to taking heed that no one deceives you. Many are going to come in the Name of Yeshua (Jesus), and they are going to deceive many. *"But he who endures to the end shall be saved" (Matthew 24.13 NKJV)*.

Following verse 13 of Matthew 24, we are told that the gospel of the kingdom shall be preached to all the world, then the end shall come when you see the Abomination of Desolation spoken of by Daniel stand in the Holy Place (Matthew 24.14-15), then shall the great tribulation such as the world has never seen (Matthew 24.21).

Yeshua says, whoever reads, let him understand: *"Therefore when you see the 'abomination of desolation,' spoken of by Daniel the prophet, standing in the holy place (whoever reads, let him understand)" (Matthew 24.15 NKJV)*. He said this because that the Abomination of Desolation spoken of in Daniel was prophetically fulfilled by Antiochus Epiphanes IV in 165-168 B.C., yet Yeshua says this will be the marker when the end shall be.

We need to look at the meaning of the word "end" in both Matthew 24.3 and Matthew 24.13 to understand what Yeshua is talking about. The word "end" in Matthew 24.3 – "What will be the sign of Your coming, and of the end of the age?" – is the Greek word *synteleia* and it's like a picture of a tail of a lion. The word "end" in Matthew 24.13 – "But he who endures to the end shall be saved" – is the Greek word *telos*, which is like the very tip of a lion's tail. Therefore, when we see the Abomination of Desolation take place, it's the beginning of the end when the world will experience the greatest tribulation that it has ever seen, and except those days be shortened, no flesh would be saved.

Add to this that *2 Thessalonians 2.3* says *"that day will not come unless the falling away comes first."* The "falling away" is the Greek word *apostasia*, which means a rebellious stand. The man of sin is revealed (apokalyptō). The son of perdition is the same as in Daniel chapters 8 and 11. He *"opposes and exalts himself above all that is called God or that sits worshiped, so he sits as God in the Temple of God showing himself as he is God" (2 Thessalonians 2.4 NKJV)*. The Abomination of Desolation is not the end, but the beginning of the end. It is when the *telos* begins. And after the tribulation, we will see the sign of Son of Man in heaven.

"[9] The coming of the lawless one is according to the working of Satan, with all power, signs, and lying wonders, [10] and with all unrighteous deception among those who perish, because they did not receive the love of the truth, that they might be saved. [11] And for this reason God will send them strong delusion, [12] that they should believe the lie" (2 Thessalonians 2.9-12 NJKV). Those who receive the love of the truth will be saved.

Personally, I'd like to simply focus on the Way and the Truth and the Life – Yeshua – and love Him only. Bridal hearts have many promises, not the least of which is that lovers of truth will be saved in the last days. The love of truth is offered as a gift to everyone. Whatever we love, whether it is love, money, or truth, we can't seem to get enough of. If we love His Truth, we will get it. You should know that "truth" will take an eternity to learn: *"And this is eternal life, that they may know You, the only true God, and Jesus Christ whom You have sent (John 17.3).* God Himself is going to be sending those who do not love the truth a strong delusion that they might believe a lie. The word "send" is the Greek word "pempō," which means to send one home to where they're comfortable. God is basically giving people the delusion they want.

Bridal hearts will want to be sent home into Yeshua's loving arms. I am not just talking about when we die. I am talking about every single minute of every single day. His pure and spotless Bride will exemplify the theme that's woven throughout Hanukkah, which is co-crucifixion with her Beloved. Never forget that a burnt offering is called an *olah* in Hebrew, which means to go up.

Discussion Questions:

1. Who is the son of perdition and is there a personal application to it?

2. What do you love the most – money, fame, food, truth?

*****

DAY 4 – Choose Beauty or the Beast

"[15] Therefore when you see the 'abomination of desolation,' spoken of by Daniel the prophet, standing in the holy place" (whoever reads, let him understand) … [21] For then there will be great tribulation, such as has not been since the beginning of the world until this time, no, nor ever shall be" (Matthew 24.15,21 NKJV).

Do you know what Yeshua was celebrating when He celebrated Hanukkah?

It could not have been the miracle of the Temple Menorah's oil lasting eight days. Nothing is spoken of this burning oil miracle for hundreds of years; and then, all of a sudden it crops up in Rabbinic literature. Since Hanukkah happened in 168-165 B.C. that means the miraculous extension of oil was made the focal point of Hanukkah after Yeshua lived here on earth, dies on the cross, was buried and rose again. What was institutional Judaism trying to hide? It has to be important, and it has to do with Yeshua's fulfillment of Hanukkah (the Feast of Dedication).

Add to that fact that over a thousand years after the celebration of Hanukkah originated, the dreidel game of chance was "sanctified" by Rabbinic decree, which was a popular German Beer Garden Spinning Top Game. The four Hebrew letters on the dreidel are said to spell out "a great miracle happened there" or "a great miracle happened here" (if you happen to be in Jerusalem). There is no doubt that a great miracle happened with Hanukkah, but what was the miracle if it wasn't finding only enough oil for one day but lasting eight days?

If you look close enough, you will find that the eight days of rejoicing during Hanukkah have to do with the re-dedication of God's Altar. Just know that God's Altar has to do with our hearts, which means the rejoicing during Hanukkah centers around the re-dedication of our hearts to worship the One True God in Spirit and in Truth (according to the Word of God).

Remember that a radical remnant withstood, and even overcame, the world-dominating Antichrist during the first Hanukkah. Many Christians seek to minimize or dismiss Hanukkah's personal application to them, but that would be a huge mistake; because Hanukkah literally holds some huge keys for the church becoming His pure and spotless Bride. Before Hanukkah happened, God tethered it to the Antichrist prophecies of Daniel three hundred years prior to the events actually happening.

After the first events of Hanukkah, Yeshua attaches a prophetic significance to the Feast of Dedication by telling us that the first Abomination of Desolation (i.e., Antichrist) is a prophetic foreshadow of an even greater abomination that confronts the believer in the last days: *"[15] Therefore when you see the 'abomination of desolation,' spoken of by Daniel the prophet, standing in the holy place" (whoever reads, let him understand) ... [21] For then there will be great tribulation, such as has not been since the beginning of the world until this time, no, nor ever shall be" (Matthew 24.15,21 NKJV).* Please refer to http://wp.me/p158HG-Gi.

Wouldn't you say that those are two major connections points to Hanukkah? If Christians value what Yeshua says about the times we are currently in; then we need to sit up and take notice. If Yeshua Himself warns people about an even greater fulfillment of the Antichrist during the end days that's connected to Hanukkah, you can bet it has to do with the focal point of the Feast of Dedication's re-dedication of God's Altar.

The first Hanukkah specifically speaks about how we are supposed to re-dedicate our hearts. In 168 B.C., corruption in the government of Judea was at an all-time high and the presiding king over Jerusalem and Judea was the Syrian-Greek (Seleucid) Antiochus Epiphanes IV. To unite all of his people and set himself up as "God," Antiochus sought to utterly annihilate the monotheistic Jewish culture and religion. In fact, had not Judah the Maccabee and his band of faithful men not taken their prolonged courageous stand against the Antichrist of their day and had they not overcome overwhelming odds, both Judaism and Christianity most likely would not exist today.

Antiochus had God's Altar desecrated on Jupiter's Winter Festival, which was the 15th day of Kislev in 168 B.C., which happened to be the 25th of December that year. The heathen put a statue of a sun god on God's Altar and sacrificed a pig on it, as a sign of utter contempt. Some people say it was a statue of Jupiter and some say it was Zeus. In a sense, it really doesn't matter, because both of them were Greek sun gods. After the dispersion from the Tower of Babel, different cultures gave different names to their sun god. Babylonian Tammuz is touted as the first sun god, but I found evidence that Nimrod claimed to be the first sun god. Ra was the Egyptian sun god. Mithra was a Persian sun god adopted by the Romans. Zeus was one of the Greek sun gods, and Jupiter another. When the Greeks under Antiochus Epiphanes IV direction set up the abomination of desolation (idol of a sun god), as foretold in the Book of Daniel, all evening and morning sacrifices ceased (Daniel 11.31; Daniel 12.11).

In 165 B.C., the fiery fulfillment of the focal point of Hanukkah happened after numerous small skirmishes with the forces that wanted to dominate the world and five major battles. Exactly three years to the day after the sun god was put upon God's Altar and a pig was sacrificed to him, the Maccabees rejoiced as they began the re-dedication of God's Altar in Jerusalem by tearing down the defiled altar and setting up a new one.

I have heard Christians and non-Christians repeatedly say that Hanukkah has nothing to do with Christmas, but that is simply not the case. Hanukkah is all about overthrowing a polluted sacrificial system instituted in God's Temple that centers around sun god worship, which is essentially Christmas. All pagan sun god birthdays were celebrated in the ancient winter solstice – December 25th. It was not a coincidence that a pagan sun god statue was erected on God's Altar that very day. Today, it is the same day that most Christians offer up the same pagan sun god deity in their hearts without knowing its origins. Your heart is God's Altar where the ultimate battle for purity is being fought.

We can read about sun god worship (Christmas) being the most detestable practice in His eyes in Ezekiel 8. *"Son of man, do you see what they are doing … things that will drive Me far from My sanctuary? (Ezekiel 8.6)* The fourth, and most detestable practice in His eyes that drives Him far from His sanctuary is in Ezekiel 8.16. People intimately acquainted with God are shown worshiping the sun. These were those who knew and loved Him, yet still grievously bowed down to the sun. Please refer to => http://wp.me/p158HG-Dx.

Yeshua did not celebrate His birth – Christmas. He celebrated Hanukkah, and the overthrow of Christmas (i.e., pagan sun god worship), Even though Jewish people have things to correct to come in line with His plumb line for the Feast of Dedication, today most Christians are actually doing what the first Antichrist did and are believing that its true and pure worship.

Let's all fulfill Hanukkah, just like Yeshua did by walking in the same manner that He did (John 10.22-23).

Discussion Questions:

1. What practices were connected to the first Hanukkah's defilement of God's Altar?

2. How do we make sure that our hearts are complete pure during the Winter One-der-land Season?

*****

DAY 5 – Mystery of Iniquity

"[7] For the mystery of lawlessness (that hidden principle of rebellion against constituted authority) is already at work in the world, [but it is] restrained only until he who restrains is taken out of the way. [8] And then the lawless one (the Antichrist) will be revealed and the Lord Jesus will slay him with the breath of His mouth and bring him to an end by His appearing at His coming" (2 Thessalonians 2.7-8 Amplified).

The mystery of the Antichrist in the first Hanukkah, which is connected the appearance of the Antichrist in our day has been sealed up until the time of the end.

As foretold in the Book of Daniel, all evening and morning sacrifices ceased in 168 B.C. (Daniel 11.31; 12.11). That day was the 15th day of Kislev (equivalent to December 25th). The city was Jerusalem. The culprit was Antiochus Epiphanes IV, who was also referred to by Yeshua as prophetic foreshadow of an even greater abomination that confronts believers in the last days: *"[15] Therefore when you see the 'Abomination of Desolation,' spoken of by Daniel the prophet, standing in the holy place (whoever reads, let him understand) … [21] For then there will be great tribulation, such as has not been since the beginning of the world until this time, no, nor ever shall be" (Matthew 24.15,21 NKJV).* By the way, this was Yeshua answer to His disciples' question: *"What shall be the sign of Thy coming, and of the end of the world* [as we know it]*?" (Matthew 24.3 comment mine).*

So, all evening and morning sacrifices ceased on December 25, 168 B.C. when Antichrist Antiochus sacrificed a pig on God's Altar and placed a sun god idol on it. You and I are the Temple of the Holy Spirit (1 Corinthians 6.19) and our hearts are his altars. Therefore, when the first Antichrist (prophesied by Daniel) set up a sun god idol on God's Altar on December 25th and sacrificed a pig to that image, it speaks of God's people making sacrifices to/for Christmas on the sun god's birthday – December 25th. This is why Yeshua celebrate Hanukkah – the overthrow of Christmas – on God's Altar, which causes the Abomination of Desolation to stand proudly in one's soul.

When we search the whole counsel of Scripture, we come up with a disturbing revelation of the Abomination of Desolation. Conveniently, Yeshua, as the embodiment of the Word of God connects the Abomination of Desolation in Matthew 24.15 to the number of the beast in Revelation 13.18 by saying "let him who has understanding." The spirit of understanding is key to unlocking this Mystery of Iniquity (2 Thessalonians 2.7), which is directly connected to *"Mystery, Babylon the Great, the mother of harlots and abominations of the earth" (Revelation 17.5 NKJV). "Here is wisdom. Let him who has understanding calculate the number of the beast, for it is the number of man: His number id 666" (Revelation 13.8 NKJV).*

The beast or the man of sin has a number. That number is the number of man without God. When we completely magnify man's enmity towards God, we understand one glaring aspect of this beast. The beast can exist within you and me, because its equivalent to a completely selfish man. The ultimate end-time battle for each of us is choosing the Kingdom of God or the Kingdom of Self. Please refer to http://wp.me/p158HG-bC.

The Mystery of Iniquity happens in the end days where there's a falling away, and the man of sin within you and I is revealed: *"Let no man deceive you by any means: for that day shall not come, except there come a falling away first, and that man of sin be revealed, the son of perdition" (2 Thessalonians 2.3 KJV)*. All Scripture can be applied personally. You and I will be on one side of the Mystery of Iniquity equation or the other. Believers will either fall away being one of the elect that can be deceived, or we will have our man of sin revealed – the parts of our carnal nature that still needs to be refined (crucified).

When Yeshua calls people to Himself in order to restore us to our pristine state, He left us with instructions: *"Whoever desires to come after Me, let him deny himself, and take up his cross, and follow Me" (Mark 8.34 NKJV)*. We are not replacing His cross, but joining Him on it. For us (on this side of the cross), we will walk in the same manner Yeshua did, except He was sinless and that's our goal. Therefore, we join Yeshua by taking up the cross of our flesh and following after Him (Matthew 10.38). Why all this cross talk? Because the cross of Christ insists on out permission to crucify our sin nature, and it is also God's sacrificial altar in our heart.

Discussion Questions:

1. What is a personal application of the Mystery of Iniquity?

2. Do you think that the Abomination of Desolation can proudly stand in your own soul? (Hint: If you think it's not possible, you are probably already deceived. We must be humble and teachable in all things.)

*****

DAY 6 – Climbing the Frequency of His Plumb Line

"Clouds and darkness are round about Him;
righteousness and judgment are the foundation of His throne"
(Psalm 97.2 Aramaic).

As we climb the frequency of His plumb line, our garments will be changed from the top down, becoming a brilliant concentrated white light. The Bide of Christ will resonate at the same frequency as her Beloved Heavenly

Bridegroom.

As a friend and I sat discussing "righteousness," we felt the Holy Spirit come. We both immediately saw that we were before this gigantic golden plumb line hanging by His frequency. His frequency looked like a white DNA strand of light, except for a thin red line that started on the right and stayed in that position as it followed the heavenly double-helix structure.

As we stood before His plumb line, we bent to the right. We were being righteously judges to see if we aligned with His plumb line. Then we heard three Big Ben booms and the Blood in His frequency set us upright. We immediately began to climb the frequency holding onto His plumb line. In fact, it was by the Blood of the Lamb that we had the grace to climb higher.

As we climbed, our garments changed from top to bottom. Our garments were not made of a material, but something otherworldly. They became as a white light all over – a brilliant concentrate white light.

We realized that as we climbed His plumb line of righteousness that our inner line was becoming one with His plumb line frequency. In fact, the encouragement we received from Love was to keep climbing higher to become one with Him. This was literally a picture of several Scriptures that He had laid on my heart:

[1] *"I press on toward the goal for the prize of the UPWARD call of God in Christ Jesus (Philippians 3.14 NASB).*

[2] *"For He made Him who knew no sin to be sin fir us, that* WE MIGHT BECOME THE RIGHTEOUSNESS OF GOD IN HIM" *(2 Corinthians 5.21 NKJV).*

[3] *"[16] Therefore thus saith the Lord GOD, Behold, I lay in Zion for a foundation a stone, a tried stone, a precious stone, a sure foundation: he that believeth shall not make haste. [17] Judgment also will I lay to the line, and* RIGHTEOUSNES TO THE PLUMMET: *and the hail shall sweep away the refuge of lies. And the waters shall overflow the hiding place" Isaiah 28.16-17 KJV).*

If Paul declared toward the end of his ministry that he needed to press on toward the goal of the upward call of God in Christ Jesus, it's a really good indicator that this is something believers still need to do too. We need to strive to enter His rest, which is literally becoming the righteousness of God in Christ Jesus here on earth, as it is in heaven. When we look at the heavenly position, which is the goal of our upward call, we are the righteousness of God in Christ Jesus. When each of us look at our current earthly condition in this regard most, if not all of us, currently fall short.

In this Kingdom Day, this perfect work of us becoming the righteousness of God in Christ Jesus will happen.

Please don't beat yourself up or get into a perfectionist mode. I've seen too many people disqualify themselves from the Bridal Race by them being too hard on themselves. "Perfect" in this context means to set out for a definite point or goal. It's the point aimed at as a limit. That limit is our beautiful Lord of Love, which is Christ in you, the hope of glory. Let us embrace the great grace provided by His Blood and climb heavenly heights that will result in our being made into His glorious image.

Discussion Questions:

1. What point are you aiming at in your spiritual life?

2. How do you measure yourself against God's plumb line?

*****

DAY 7 – Golden Scribe Angel

"And Enoch found favor in the presence of God, and disappeared; for God took him away" (Genesis 5.24 Aramaic).

Our heavenly Father has graciously commanded a golden scribe angel to come forth from His angelic beehive. What should have taken me months, took me one week to write – the booklet called the *Blazing New Wine of Hanukkah: Bridal Restoration of DNA*. I'm truly amazed at His goodness and grace. I am also shocked at how revelatory it is and how bold! Go God!!!

Years ago, when I had just finished writing the *SANTA-TIZING: What's wrong with Christmas and how to clean it up* in conjunction with a golden scribe angel, Yeshua put me in a silver boxcar time machine and transported me to the future where I was saw a dead man laying down with Santa Claus boots on. When I peered around the boots, I saw that it was actually Santa Claus with only a couple mourners around him, which I somehow knew represented all of Christmas. Then I looked to my right and saw Yeshua being highly exalted and praised by a great throng of people.

It's time for His Bride to come forth!!! Let your YES be "Yes," your NO be "No." By the way, everything lukewarm goes into the "No" category. I used to love Christmas myself, and I mean love… until Yeshua showed up epiphaneously three times. The first time Yeshua came to me with tears in His eyes and told Me: "The mixture of Christmas grieves My heart." He paused to let that bombshell sink in; then added: "Come out of Babylon and lay down Christmas for I will have a pure and spotless

Bride." My family and I laid down Christmas that year. Yeshua's second epiphaneous appearance was about a year later when He came to me and literally married me by putting a ring on my finger. Then, the third time He appeared, He asked me to tell the Christian Church that "Christmas will be the Golden Calf of America." I wrote the book *SANTA-TIZING: What's wrong with Christmas and how to clean it up* to fulfill this vow that I made three times to His face.

I was amazed when God told me that the Golden Scribe Angel was actually Enoch as Metatron! The prominent scribal office of Enoch in Merkabah form! This concept is also revealed in *Sepher Hekhalot* (*Book of Palaces*, also known as the *Third Book of Enoch*) where it recounts an ascent and divine transformation of the biblical figure Enoch into his cherubic Metatron form.

The *Targum Pseudo-Jonathan* translation of *Genesis 5.24* reads: *"Enoch worshiped in truth before the Lord, and behold he was not with the inhabitants of the earth because he was taken away and he ascended to the firmament at the command of the Lord, and he was called Metatron, the Great Scribe."*

References to Enoch's scribal duties can be found in the books of 1 Enoch and Jubilees. *Jubilees 4.23* refers to a particular dimension of Enoch's ascension: *"We conduct him into the Garden of Eden in majesty and honor, and behold there he writes down the condemnation and judgment of the world, and all the wickedness of the children of man."*

This is the Golden Scribe Angel that our Heavenly Father mercifully sent to me to help write the books: *SANTA-TIZING: What's wrong with Christmas and how to clean it up* (https://www.amazon.com/SANTA-TIZING-Whats-wrong-Christmas-clean/dp/1607911159) and *Blazing New Wine of Hanukkah: Bridal Restoration of DNA* (https://www.amazon.com/Blazing-Wine-Hanukkah-Bridal-Restoration/dp/1634430026).

Remember that God's heart is for mercy to always triumph over judgment (James 2.13). Never forget the Judge is the Door of Life. Therefore, all of God's judgements are actually mercy, because He only judges things not in agreement with love, life and light.

Different pictures of the Merkabah form of Enoch – Metatron – reveal various aspects to this Golden Scribe Angel's heavenly function. Do your own research. The Great Scribe Metatron is pictured as having a seat or throne in heaven, as an enthroned cherubic scribe. He writes down the merits of Israel and is said to be an assistant of the Deity in divine judgment. In other words, Enoch-Metatron is ruling and reigning alongside the Holy One of Israel: *"At first I sat upon a great throne at the door of the seventh palace, and I judged all the denizens of the heights on the authority of the Holy One, blessed be He … when I sat in the heavenly court. The princes of kingdoms stood beside me, to my right and to my left, by authority of the Holy One, blessed be He. But when Acher came to behold the vision of the chariot and set eyes upon me, he was afraid and trembled before me. His soul was alarmed to the point of leaving him, because of his fear, dread, and terror of me, when he saw me seated upon a throne like a king, with ministering angels standing beside me as servants and all the princes of kingdoms crowned with crowns surrounding me" (3 Enoch 16).*

This picture of the Merkabah form of Melchizedek Enoch is also a picture for those who will be taken by God, like Enoch, and for those mature into the fullness of the Order of Melchizedek being literally made into the exact same image as Messiah Yeshua (Jesus Christ) here on earth, as it is in heaven.

Not only does Enoch operate as the Merkabah Metatron – a judge in God's heavenly courts – so do other generals in His Melchizedek Army as directed by the High Priest of the Order Himself (Yeshua). Yes, Enoch-Metatron is a heavenly scribe. Thank God for his assistance! I have had a holy, reverential fear in writing these books, since I made a vow three times to Yeshua's face to tell the Christian Church that "Christmas will be the Golden Calf of America."

I have wondered all those years how I could fully hit the perfect mark of God in this high calling. Now I know. I alone could not. I have continually stormed His Throne of Grace asking Him to please help me. You can press in too. Press in and never give up!

We give Him all the glory and honor and praise!

Source: "Metatron as the Scribe" by Andrei A. Orlov [an excerpt from A. Orlov, The Enoch-Metatron Tradition (TSAJ, 107; Tuebingen: Mohr-Siebeck, 2005), pp. xii+383. ISBN 3-16-148544-0.]

Discussion Questions:

1. Why was Enoch taken by God?

2. What is Enoch's heavenly scribe function?

*****

DAY 8 – Yeshua's Full Government Declaration

"Jesus said to them, 'Most assuredly, I say to you, before Abraham was, I AM'" (John 8.58 NKJV).

It is significant that Yeshua governmental declares "I AM" twelve time during Hanukkah before the John 10.22-23 reference to Yeshua celebrating Hanukkah:

- *"Then Jesus spoke to them again, saying, "I AM THE LIGHT OF THE WORLD. He who follows Me shall not walk in darkness, but have the light of life" (John 8.12 NKJV).*

- *"And He said to them, 'You are from beneath; I AM FROM ABOVE. You are of this world; I AM NOT OF THIS WORLD" (John 8.23 NKJV).*

- *"Then Jesus said to them, 'WHEN YOU LIFT UP THE SON OF MAN, THEN YOU WILL KNOW THAT I AM, and I do nothing of Myself; but as My Father taught Me, I speak these things" (John 8.28 NKJV).*

- *"Jesus said to them, 'Most assuredly, I say to you, BEFORE ABRAHAM WAS, I AM'" (John 8.58 NKJV).*

- *"AS LONG AS I AM IN THE WORLD, I AM THE LIGHT OF THE WORLD" (John 9.5 NKJV).*

- *"Then Jesus said to them again, 'Most assuredly, I say to you, I AM THE DOOR of the sheep'" (John 10.7 NKJV).*

- *"I AM THE DOOR, If anyone enters by Me, he will be saved, and will go in and out and find pasture" (John 10.9 NKJV).*

- *"The thief cometh not, but to steal, and to kill, and to destroy: IAM COME THAT THEY MIGHT HAVE LIFE, and that they might have it more abundantly" (John 10.10 NKJV).*

- *"I AM THE GOOD SHEPHERD. The good shepherd gives His life for the sheep" (John 10.11 NKJV).*

- *"I AM THE GOOD SHEPHERD; and I know My sheep, and am known by My own" (John 10.14 NKJV).*

Please do not underestimate that Scripture records that Yeshua walked in the Temple in Solomon's Porch during the Feast of Dedication (Hanukkah). If you want to be made into the same image as Yeshua, you will walk as He walked. In fact, when my family came out of the Yuletide Season based in Babylon, Yeshua told me to do what He did when I forlornly asked Him what to do to replace the big hole that was in our family after laying down Christmas.

Biblical Feasts are the crux for the manifestation of one flock and one shepherd (John 10.16), or in other words, the One New Man in the messiah (Ephesians 2.15). Please refer to http://wp.me/p158HG-Dx.

After the reference to Yeshua celebrating Hanukkah in John 10.22-23, there is one more of Yeshua's "I AM" statements making a governmental declaration into one of full government (13 = 12 disciples + Yeshua): *"If He called them gods, to whom the Word of God came (and the Scripture cannot be broken), do you say to Him whom the Father sanctified and sent into the world, 'You are blaspheming,' because I said, 'I AM THE SON OF GOD?'" (John 10.35-36 NKJV).* Hebrews 7.3 tells us that those that are made after the Order of Melchizedek are made like unto the Son of God. Therefore, in full government declaration in John 10.36, we can see a reference to a people that all creation is waiting for (Romans 8.19). They are the mature sons of the Most High God that the Father sanctifies and sends into the world.

Discussion Questions:

1. What Hanukkah I AM statements speak to you?

2. Why is the manifestation of the sons of God connected to Yeshua's Full Government?

*****

9 – KINDLING OF HANUKKAH LIGHTS

The Temple Menorah was a golden, seven-branch lampstand. The Hanukkah/Chanukah menorah has nine branches instead of seven. Eight of these branches remember the eight days of Hanukkah and one is called the *shammus* – servant candle – which is used to light the other candles. (It's a prophetic picture of Jesus humbling Himself by coming into the world as a servant and as the Light of the World.)

If you don't have a Hanukkah Menorah (i.e., *Hanukkiah* in Hebrew), you can pull together a make-shift one. Simply get nine separate candles (tea lights, pillars, or other) and put eight of them together. Set the other one apart or higher than the others. (Those of you who are arts and crafts people will love getting creative with this.)

The lighting of the Hanukkah candles is a simple

tradition that commemorates the eight days that it took to cleanse God's Altar and re-dedicate His Temple. The object of lighting the Menorah is to publicize God's miracle of His people defeating the Antichrist of their day. This is something happening in our day as well.

Hanukkah candles have been traditionally placed near windows to remind others of the Hanukkah miracles and His people's redemption. Know that the lighting of the Hanukkah candles is only a ritual to remind people of God's greatness and grace, so don't get too anxious about the details (and at the same time realize the details speak of profound truths.)

The most widely followed custom on the first night of Hanukah is: First strike a match and light the *shammus* candle. Blow out the match. (Be sure to look away from the *hanukkiah* when you blow out the match.) Then take the shammus candle to kindle the candle to the extreme right of the person lighting the lamp. On the second night one adds a light to the left of the first one, kindles the added light first and then, moves to their right. This procedure is repeated every night (first one kindles the added light and then one kindles the rest by moving left to right).

*****

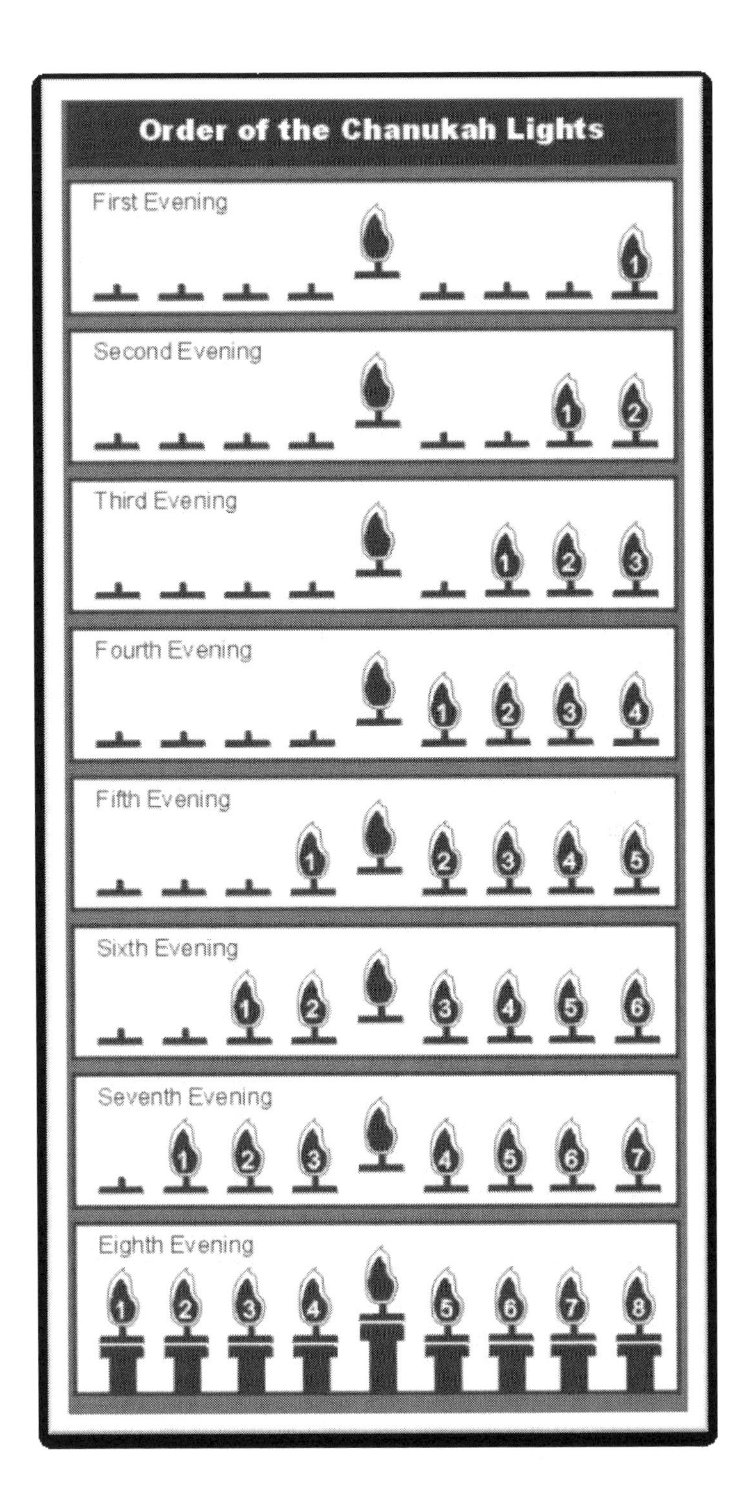
Order of the Chanukah Lights
First Evening
1
Second Evening
1 2
Third Evening
1 2 3
Fourth Evening
1 2 3 4
Fifth Evening
1 2 3 4 5
Sixth Evening
1 2 3 4 5 6
Seventh Evening
1 2 3 4 5 6 7
Eighth Evening
1 2 3 4 5 6 7 8

10 – NIGHTY BLESSINGS

As the Hanukkah candles are lit, a blessing is spoken over them. The first night a special blessing is usually said to open the festive season of our joy with another blessing following it.

You can say your own blessings from your heart that's related to the re-dedication of your heart, or you can use the ones provided below.

A general guideline for kindling lights is given below for the first day of Hanukah; then an general guideline is given for the second to eighth days of Hanukkah. Remember the first night of Hanukkah differs slightly due to the opening of Hanukkah. Know that all of these blessings are simply examples.

On the first night of Hanukkah, follow these directions:

DAY 1:

1. "Blessed are you, Lord our God, King of the universe, who sanctifies us. Blessed are you, Lord our God, who is the Light of the world. We bless your most holy name as we kindle these Chanukah lights."

2. "Blessed are you, Lord our God, King of the universe, who does miracles. We remember your miracles performed at this season in days of old."

3. "Blessed are you, Lord our God, King of the universe, who has preserved us and enabled us to reach this season."

4. Light the candles.

5. After kindling the lights, say:

   "We kindle these lights to commemorate the saving acts, miracles, and wonders that you have performed. We also look forward to seeing miracles, signs, and wonders in our day. Throughout the eight days of Chanukah, these lights are sacred. They are not meant for a common purpose. We only look upon these lights in order to offer You thanks and praise to Your great Name."

The following are the general directions for the blessing said while kindling the Hanukkah lights:

DAY 2 – DAY 8:

1. "Blessed are you, Lord our God, King of the universe, who sanctifies us. Blessed are you, Lord our God, who is the Light of the world. We bless your most holy name as we kindle these Hanukkah lights."

2. "Blessed are you, Lord our God, King of the universe, who does miracles. We remember your miracles performed at this season in days of old."

3. Light the candles.

4. After kindling the lights, say:

   "We kindle these lights to commemorate the saving acts, miracles, and wonders that you have performed. We also look forward to seeing miracles, signs, and wonders in our day. Throughout the eight days of Hanukkah, these lights are sacred. They are not meant for a common purpose. We only look upon these lights in order to offer You thanks and praise to Your Great Name."

*****

ALTERNATE FIRST NIGHT BLESSING:

“Blessed are You, O Lord our God, King of the Universe, who granted us life, sustained us and permitted us to reach this season.”

TRADITIONAL BLESSING:

“Blessed are You, O Lord our God, King of the universe, who has sanctified us with Your commandments, and commanded us to light Hanukkah lights.”

Blessed are You, O Lord our God, King of the universe, who performed miracles for our fathers in those days at this season.”

BUILDING UP FAITH BLESSING:

“Blessed are You, O Lord our God, King of the universe, who has given us holidays, customs, and times of happiness, to increase the knowledge of God and to build up our most holy faith.”

“Blessed are You, O Lord our God, King of the universe, who performed miracles for our fathers in those days at this season.”

RE-DEDICATION OF THE ALTAR BLESSING:

"Blessed are You, O Lord our God, King of the universe, you are worthy, worthy, worthy of pure and holy worship."

"Blessed are You, O Lord our God, King of the universe, we re-dedicate our hearts solely to You, our First Love. We choose from our very depths to purify our temples as You, the Good Shepherd, chooses.

*****

ABOUT THE AUTHOR

Robin Main is a prophetic artist, author, speaker and teacher who equips people to be the unique and beautiful creation that they have been created to be. She flows in love, revelation and wisdom with her SPECIALTY being kingdom enlightenment.

Her MISSION is to enlighten the nations by venturing to educate and restore the sons of the Living God.

Her CALL is a clarion one to mature sons and the pure and spotless Bride who will indeed be without spot or wrinkle.

Her ULTIMATE DESIRE is that everyone be rooted and grounded in love, so they can truly know the height, width, breadth and width of the Father's love.

Made in the USA
San Bernardino, CA
18 January 2017